CW01459731

You're Your Father's Daughter

Fr. Mark Ngwah

Published by Mark Ngwah, 2024.

YOU'RE YOUR FATHER'S DAUGHTER

First edition. February 14, 2024.

Copyright © 2024 Fr. Mark Ngwah.

ISBN: 979-8224387564

Written by Fr. Mark Ngwah.

FR   MARK NDIFOR OFM CAP.

YOU'RE YOUR FATHER'S DAUGHTER

"If you think fathers are not important ask any child who doesn't have one"

Book Description.

Ever felt the echo of a missing hand in yours? The sting of a chair perpetually empty at the table? In "You're Your Father's Daughter," we delve into the often-ignored realm of father absence, its impact on daughters, and the journey to self-discovery that follows.

From the opening, "If you think fathers are not important ask any child who doesn't have one," we confront the profound influence fathers wield. We dissect the meaning of fatherhood, its inception, and the very question: are fathers truly necessary?

Fr Mark Ndifor OFM Cap, expertly dissects the complex phenomenon of absent fathers, dedicating chapters to understanding the various types of absences, their prevalence in specific regions like Kenya, and the underlying causes that contribute to this heartbreaking reality.

Challenging societal assumptions, Fr Mark Ndifor OFM Cap explores the limitations of mothers filling the paternal void and asks the crucial question: can a mother truly teach her son how to be a man?

The chapters pulsate with the raw emotions of fatherless children. We hear the echoes of "Daddy issues!" the sting of "Where's my daddy?", and the constant questioning of why absentee fathers impact daughters more than sons. We tackle the myth of mothers teaching sons how to be men and navigate the complex reality of being "Your Father's child," even in his absence.

But "You're Your Father's Daughter" is not merely a lament. It is a beacon of hope, a roadmap to overcoming father absence and forging your own path. Through chapters like "Making it without a father" and

3

"Positive Self-Talk for daughters with absent and unknown fathers," we equip you with the tools to heal, to thrive, and to reclaim your narrative.

This book is a powerful call to action for fathers, would-be fathers, and absent fathers alike. It is a reminder of the profound impact they have, and a plea to embrace their roles with love and responsibility.

"You're Your Father's Daughter" is more than a book, it's a conversation starter, a healing balm, and a celebration of the resilience and strength that blossoms even in the face of absence.

Are you ready to reclaim your story? Dive in and discover the daughter you were always meant to be.

About the Author

Fr. Mark Ndifor OFM Cap is a dedicated Catholic priest belonging to the Franciscan Capuchin Friars. With a profound commitment to serving his community, Fr. Mark has spent over two decades in priesthood, embodying the values of compassion, empathy, and service.

Fr. Mark holds a Master of Arts degree in Counseling Psychology, earned through diligent study and dedication to understanding the complexities of the human psyche. His academic journey also includes a Bachelor of Arts in Counseling Studies from the University of Manchester, as well as a Higher Diploma in Counseling Studies. He is a registered member of the Kenya Association of Professional Counselors, showcasing his commitment to upholding the highest standards of professional practice in his field.

During his academic pursuits, Fr. Mark delved deep into the intricacies of father absence and its impact on daughters' self-esteem. His master dissertation, titled **"Influence of Absentee Fathers on Daughters' Self-Esteem in Selected Colleges in Ruiru Sub-County, Kiambu County, Kenya,"** sheds light on this crucial subject, offering valuable insights into the challenges faced by young women in the absence of paternal guidance.

As Fr. Mark celebrates his 25th year in priesthood, marking a remarkable silver jubilee in his service to God and community, he continues to be a beacon of hope and support for those in need. His unwavering dedication to helping others navigate the complexities of life has earned him respect and admiration from all who know him.

Acknowledgment:

I extend my heartfelt gratitude to Dr. Catherine Kirimi for her unwavering support and valuable guidance throughout the journey of completing my book, "YOU'RE YOUR FATHER'S DAUGHTER." Her expertise and encouragement have been instrumental in shaping and refining my work.

I am deeply appreciative of Dr. Gilbert Maroko for his insightful feedback and dedicated efforts in rephrasing and reshaping my topic. His contributions have added a layer of depth and clarity to my work that I am truly grateful for.

A special thanks goes to Dr. Florence K'Okul for her guidance and unwavering support, which played a crucial role in the successful completion of my book. Her encouragement and mentorship have been invaluable, and I am truly fortunate to have had her by my side throughout this process.

I am grateful to have had the privilege of working with such esteemed individuals, and their contributions have significantly enriched the quality of my work. Thank you for your invaluable support and mentorship.

Feedback

This book offers a solid framework for an admirable, independently researched master-piece of its own kind. It is captivating to the reader moving from one page to another where the content leaves one craving to hear more. The fact that the author tackles "Father daughter relationship" an area that hasn't received enough attention in research studies makes it outstanding at a glance. It is for this sole reason that 1 recommends it to parents, guardians and child-caregivers especially in the current generation where father's absence is a rapid phenomenon. Thank you.

Gabriel Kauru Peter
Senior Clinical Supervisor.
Mathari National Teaching & Referral Hospital
. Nairobi-Kenya

Father daughter relationship

"Individuals have numerous significant relationships throughout their lifespan, however, the most important relationship one may have in a lifetime is a relationship of a child with father/ parents. The child and father relationship leads towards a unique bond that plays an influentially crucial role in a child's life." (Farooqi R & Khan A, 2021)

THE PSYCHOTHERAPIST'S PERSPECTIVE

"From time to time, most psychotherapists find themselves confronted in their practice with clients who do not know one of their genetic parents. In the overwhelming majority of cases, this is their genetic father" (Terwogt M, Reijnders, C J & . Hekken ML, 2002)

"This phenomenon of children growing up without knowing their biological fathers is not going to go away soon". (Nduna M & Jewkes R, 2010)

"Girls are most affected by fatherlessness since it influences how they socialize. Men are biologically trained to be independent, so separation and isolation do not change them as much as it affects the girl child. The man can ignore feelings; the woman, on the other hand, obsesses about feelings, which leads her to behaviors such as staying in relationships too long and searching for "the perfect man." The girl may also attempt to become a "superwoman," effectively trying to pretend she does not love or need others for her survival" (Smith K A, 2017)

"The common assumption has been that children from father-absent families do not achieve success in life. However, many examples exist of children who have grown up in father absent families becoming productive members of society" (Smith K A, 2017)

PREFACE

Father daughter relationship has been an interest of mine for quite sometimes may be because while growing up 1 realized that the relationship between my dad and elder sister was not a very good one. This resonated with what my psych prof said to us:

> *"May be when you chose psychology, there was something ... wrong with you.... Something troubling you. And maybe you came here to look for people who were like you. And you looked around and realized everyone was crazy here" I felt that.*

> *"People who become obsessed with psychology and personality types are children who were never understood at home*

> *They try to understand you with every detail, because it would mean the world to them if someone would have done the same for them. It's a love language."*

An Embarrassing topic

My aim is not to stigmatized daughters with absentee fathers but to raise awareness of the challenges they encounter and suggest coping skills. The work is not only useful to daughters with absent fathers but for all. If you're not a dad of a daughter, please continue to read on anyway. Why? Because it's highly likely that you're married to a daughter (remember your wife is a daughter), and that your son will one day marry a daughter. The work is also very useful to counselors:

> **Professional counselors are obligated to remain current with societal changes regarding family structure in order to be effective in assisting families through transitions and times of stress. Divorce, delaying marriage or opting out of a legal marriage, remarriage, (La Guardia AC, . Nelson J A & Lertora I M, 2014)**

While collecting data for my master thesis on: (Influence of absentee fathers on daughter's self-esteem in selected colleges in Ruiru- sub country Kiambu country, Kenya,) I had a tough time recruiting students with absent fathers. Many of them found it extremely uncomfortable disclosing in public that they are from absent father's homes. This resonated with the following statement:

> The topic of the 'genetic father' might be a taboo if there are strong feelings of shame: shame about not growing up in a 'normal' family or shame about being rejected by one of the parents. When attempting to address the issue of the absent

11

father it is therefore necessary to be aware of the possibility that the resistance to this topic may be very strong, unless the topic is approached with the utmost care. If the mother, out of feelings of embarrassment and/or aggression against her former partner, bars or misrepresents information about him, then she is the one who frustrates the child's desire for a father. The child quickly learns that 'the father' is a topic that is best avoided (unless he or she wants to risk punishment in the form of problems with the mother). It is apparently an embarrassing topic, which is also better not discussed with friends who have a 'normal' father. The child therefore remains alone with the cherished image of the father. . In some cases, the mother refuses to talk about her former partner and in other cases it is obvious that as a result of her own frustration with the broken relationship she can provide only a very biased view of the father. Again, the child will resort to fantasies in an attempt to correct this one-sided picture. A number of people discover only very late in life that (Terwogt M, Reijnders, C J & . Hekken ML, 2002)"

The meaning of fatherhood

"**F**athers have long been the forgotten parent, and daughters the forgotten offspring" (A, Skordas M, 1988)

There is no universally accepted definition of fatherhood, therefore different researchers have varied perspectives (Makofane M, 2015)

What does it mean to be a father? it is also a question that throughout the world and history has been largely neglected. Father has often been termed "The Forgotten Parent" In the past, our society has traditionally thought of fathers as the financial providers or breadwinners for their families (THORNE D R, 2001) Concerns about sexism have often meant that the role of fathers has been sidelined in discussions about children, in favor of emphasizing the mother (O'Dwyer D, 2017)

Fatherhood is still a concept that resides on the periphery of parenthood, despite recent discourse that acknowledges the necessity for fathers and emphasizes the significance of active fathers on the positive outcomes of their children (Thompson A, 2014).

The word "father" conjures up several images to a young person such as that of a powerful male who will love, protect, and provide her/his needs. Traditionally, fathers have been seen as providers, (ATM fathers) guardians, role models, contributors and disciplinarians rarely as nurturer (Makofane M, 2015)

These ideas are, however, being challenged in contemporary society. Many men who are fathers now work in occupations that their fathers, and particularly their grandfathers, would not have undertaken only a few years ago. According to dominant conceptions of modern parenting, fathers participate in activities that were previously only the mothers' domain. The most noticeable improvements to "update" how people view fathers have included things like cooking, cleaning, and helping to nurture and guide their child (Thompson A, 2014).

There is a communitarian spirit present in the traditional African context. "father" is not necessarily exclusive to the biological father but can also apply to other males from the extended family such as the younger and older brother of the father.

Africans believe that every adult has a right to raise a kid, thus even in the absence of biological dads, children should still be safeguarded and cared for (Gladys T R, 2020)

In African culture, the concept of community or social fathering is pervasive. If a biological father neglects his child, the child does not necessarily become fatherless. There is no such thing as a fatherless child, and the fact that a child does not live with or only occasionally sees their biological father does not change that reality. The physical role of the father is filled by other males in the family, such as grandfathers, stepfathers, foster fathers, older brothers, relatives, or family friends. Regardless of genetics, communities have a common (Thompson A, 2014).

When does fatherhood begins

Teacher: How old is your father?
Kid: He is 6 years
Teacher: what? How is this possible?
Kid: He became father only when l was born
(Logic): Children are quick and always speak their minds

When men's transitional experiences as fathers and mothers' transitional experiences are compared, it becomes clear that: Mothers reinforce their identities as mothers through the stories they tell with other mothers. From stories of experiences that women have during gestation to birth, women are more likely to tell and retell these stories and thus reinforce their roles as mothers. Fathers on the other hand, simply do not engage typically in these types of conversations with their friends.

Furthermore, beyond the physical changes that a woman goes through, there are other external factors that serve as reminders that emphasize the transition to motherhood such as, baby showers, maternity clothes, prenatal appointments and advice about mothering, with birth being the culmination of the transformation. Since men do not biologically experience pregnancy, the transition period is often neglected and leaves men feeling separated from the entire process. This alienation prevents them from being connected to their new identity as fathers although some expectant fathers want to participate in and experience pregnancy and birth

In order to connect with their new identities as fathers, they need to learn about pregnancy, birth and parenting by reading and talking to others. More suggestions for fostering this new identity and transitional period include: ensuring physical and emotional health, attending prenatal appointments, developing a connection to the baby while in utero, supporting their partners and helping to make important decisions throughout pregnancy and birth and finally, attending prenatal classes. (Thompson A, 2014).

Are father's necessary?

SOME WOMEN SAY THEY DON'T NEED A MAN. BUT I DON'T CARE WHAT THEY SAY...

OUR CHILDREN NEED THEIR FATHERS

Most recent research demonstrates that too many fathers are demeaned, demoralized and disenfranchised. Some unmarried women who choose to be artificially inseminated by anonymous sperm donors do not believe that fathers are necessary for the wellbeing of their children (Nielen L, 2012)

All children need affirmation from the fathers.

"You are my beloved Son (Daughter) in whom, I am well pleased." Mk 1:11

Just Jesus received confirmation and validation from his heavenly farther on the day of his baptism so to all human being need validation.

We all need Attention, affection affirmation, these three A's from our fathers. Failure to get this we will seek them out from another masculine source... from outside of the home... from someone whose motives are less noble and honorable... who's more interested in receiving life for himself, rather than offering life to another

Every person needs the blessing from their fathers,

> *"If most ladies had their fathers bold enough to talk to them they will be very successful in their marriage and they will be very happy people. Most women have never been taught by their fathers in particular. That is their biggest problem. They don't know who a man is they think he is another woman"*

Most adults still struggle today, low self-esteem, working all the time trying to prove they are good enough all because of their father's lack of affirmation. Their father never told them I'm proud of you, he never made them feel approved so they are still trying to measure up gain approval that can only come from the father. *A father is the daughter's mirror. Without a father there is a loss of mirroring. The grandiose self is an aspect of self that "wants to feel special and full of well-being" and needs to be mirrored by "people who will reflect and identify its unique capacities, talents* (Varney-Wong A, 2019)

> *"if a father makes his daughter feels like she is THE princess she is the most wonderful special girl in the world then it really makes her strong and feel good about herself and help her to have a great self-image and therefore when some boy comes along says wow you're really special she is like yeah l know that uh if it doesn't happen and some boy come along and blows in her ears and says you're really special: oooh really and she just leans in there like oh my God. I have been waiting all my whole to hear that. The*

fact of the matter is your dad is not in the picture at this point and that makes you kind of vulnerable"

Father have something to give their children that nobody else can give. Other people can tell them how great they are; how special they are but when you tell them it carries a whole new weight. As a father you have a God given authority to bless your child, every time you say I'm proud of your I love you, you are beautiful. God releases strength into your child value confidence security those are not just nice words it's what the scripture calls the blessing you are propelling your child toward their destiny. We are all busy it's easy to get sidetrack or even at odds with our children and they are not doing right when they straighten up I will be nicer when I am not so busy I will spend more time with them or Joel they know I am proud of them. I told them 14 years ago when we brought them home from the hospital, no they need to hear again and again. You are the father you carry the blessing, don't withhold your love your affection your approval now you may not have received this blessing from your father he wasn't around growing up or maybe he was there but all he did was correct you, tell you what you are doing wrong he didn't show affection make you feel valuable don't let that negative cycle get passed to the next generation you can be the difference make you can set a new standard start blessing your children start calling their seeds of greatness them what they can become, prophesying their future . Let them know you are their number one fan. When you see them in the morning give them a hug, Don't let them pass by with showing them your affection sometimes we were raised to think we're men. We don't express our feelings we don't hug we don't say nice things that would make us look weak. It's just the opposite when you show your feelings you are strong. Real men hug their children; real men show affection make their children feel valuable Real men go out of their way to approve to validate to encourage Father our children have been given to us as a gift

MOTHER IS GOLD, FATHER IS MIRROR,

A **GOOD FATHER** IS ONE OF THE MOST **UNSUNG, UNPRAISED, UNNOTICED,** AND YET ONE OF THE MOST **VALUABLE** ASSETS IN OUR SOCIETY.

BILLY GRAHAM

The pic says a lot about
the father's effort,
but the kid only see's the mother's love.

MY FIRST ROOM MY MOM'S WOMB
MY FIRST RESTAURANT MY MOM'S BREAST
MY FIRST TOILET MY MOM'S LAP
MY FIRST SCHOOL MY MOM'S KITCHEN
MY FIRST DOCTOR MY MON'S
MY FIRST THERMOMETER MY MOM'S FINGER
MY FIRST FRIEND MY MOTHER/

THE FATHER-DAUGHTER relationship is usually more damaged than the father-son relationship Because mothers and daughters tend to confide more in each other, daughters, more likely than sons, turn against the father and form an alliance with the mother when things are not going well in the marriage (Nielen L, 2012)

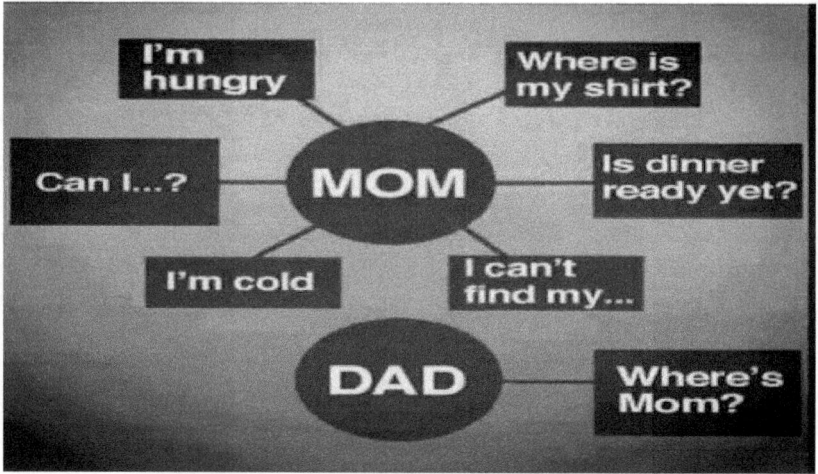

"The woman is somebody who is supposed to take care for the child. They are born to do that. She is responsible in any way for the child. When a child cries, he does not say "Papa". He says "Mama", from a young age. When he starts to talk he says "Mama". Women are responsible for the social well-being of the children. And we are responsible for financial well-being of the child. If we can change and say that I'm guarding the child. I nappy him, I bath him and I say that the woman must go and look for a job, it won't work. It will look like we are crazy; it will seem like the nation is going crazy".

Defining father absence

The term "father absence" is ambiguous because all parents occasionally spend time apart from their kids. Moreover, there are very few definitions of this phrase in the literature. Because of the lack of definitional clarity, the term 'father absence' can encompass a range of circumstances, including having a father who is non-existent in one's life, lost through death, divorce or family discord, absent through work commitments, , employed in the military, travel regularly for business and live away from their children for extended periods of time, absent from the family residence due to incarceration or institutionalization, or physically present yet absent due to disinterest or neglect

Distinction between different types of father absence

1)Absent and unknown fathers

"There is no worse pain than not knowing your father"

Unknown fathers: Means the child has no knowledge. Might be the child was very young when the father died or left so there is no recollection of the fathers because there was little or no interaction. A father is also unknown when the mother of the child doubts or does not want to reveal the identity or name of the father. The mother of the child might not be willing to give information or the name of the child's father for purposes of official registration. (Padi T,Nduna M, Khunou G, & Kholopane, 2014)

Unknown fathers do not also necessarily mean that a child completely ignorant about information concerning the father. Some child may have insight that may not be enough for them to say they know their father fully. Some may clandestinely acquire information from other people outside family or by eavesdropping from other adults (Nduna M, 2014)

2)Absent and undisclosed fathers

An undisclosed father: When the mother refuses to tell or reveal to the child who the father is. The mother may also give incorrect information. The mother's unwillingness to disclosed the child's father due denied pregnancy, incest, impregnated by married man or the mother wishes to have no contact with the father of the child. (Padi T,Nduna M, Khunou G, & Kholopane, 2014) Where the relationship was short-lived or a single encounter some mothers have little or not enough information to share with the child. In some cases, due the frustration with the broken relationship with the former partner some mother refuses to talk about him to the kids (Terwogt, Terwogt-Reijnders,, & Hekken , 2002).

3)Absent but known fathers

The absent but known father is a father one is staying with but feels they know very little about him as a result of the lack of a relationship between them. Lack of interaction and communication with the father, even in cases where he is known, accounted for a perception of him as unknown. The idea of knowing one's father entails more than just knowing his identity. A father who is known but does not play a role in one's raising, is paradoxically described as 'unknown'. This seemed to indicate the necessity of developing a closer, more meaningful bond with the absent fathers (Padi T,Nduna M, Khunou G, & Kholopane, 2014):

4) Unknown deceased fathers

Refers to a deceased father who was not known. The father might have passed away when one was still very young and have no memories of him.

'He passed away while I was young .... I don't know him because the time he passed away I was only 4 years old"

Where details and story of a deceased father are unknown to the child the father is regarded as unknown. It is reasonable to assume that orphans who knew their fathers and those who did not would have different perspectives on being orphaned. (Padi T,Nduna M, Khunou G, & Kholopane, 2014)

5) The fantasy father

Our genetic parents, whether they are present or absent, always function as figures of identification. (Terwogt M, Reijnders, C J & . Hekken ML, 2002)"

Father-absent children often fantasies about their father The adage "absence makes the heart grow fonder" may hold true. They frequently believe that the absence is their own fault mother (O'Dwyer D, 2017)

Characteristics of oneself that are not found in other relatives, especially the mother, can be attributed to the absent father. This results in the creation of an identification figure from whom it is difficult and for some impossible to detach oneself, due to lack of actual information. children who know very little about their procreators create their own fantasy parents. Differences that such children observe between themselves and their caregiver(s) can activate this process. The less information a child has about the genetic father, the more he/she is likely to fantasize about him and the more pronounced the occurrence of an identity problems. From time to time, the child will further be conscious of the fact that the picture of the father is solely based on fantasies. To the extent that it is possible to speak of an identity, it rests on a fantasized personality. As a result, the person experiences feelings of emptiness and confusion. The following quote from the Portuguese writer Fernando Pessoa illustrates this clearly: "Today I suddenly experienced an absurd but quite valid sensation. I realized, in an intimate lightning flash, that I am no one. No one, absolutely no one. (......) I am the outskirts of a non-existent town, a prolix commentary on an unwritten book. I don't know how to feel, how to think, how to love. I am a character in an unwritten novel, passing by, airy and unmade, without having existed, amid the dreams of whoever it is who didn't know how to complete me. (......) My soul is a black maelstrom, a vast vertigo around a vacuum, the movement of an infinite ocean around a hole in the void, and in the waters that are more a spinning than water float all the images that I have seen and heard in the world - there are houses, faces, books, boxes, musical refrains, and isolated syllables, in a sinister, bottomless whirl. (Terwogt M, Reijnders, C J & . Hekken ML, 2002)

The absent father phenomenon

Father absenteeism is a social phenomenon that is global and rampant in most communities (Fazel, 2017). It is a phenomenon that is affecting many countries worldwide, such as European countries like United State of America, African countries such as South Africa, Kenya among others countries (MUTEGI1 C k, Ndolo u, & . MWALW'A S, 2017)

Research on the significance and effect of fatherlessness can be traced back as the Second World War when studies were conducted to assess how children's development was affected by their fathers' absence. In addition, there is a study by Freud identifying father loss as the single greatest loss a person can experience (Dickerson C,, 2014).

The contemporary society is one of freedom, a society of indiscipline, one that lacks a sense of responsibility towards children, a society where Women feel empowered to take care of a child without a man. (Larcher A, 2007) .Father absence has a recorded link to the establishment of feminist movements. In the 1960s due to inequality that existed between the genders, women sought for liberation. They initiated the decline of male traditional role and bringing about chaos in the role men in society. They came up with slogans like: "we don't need them (men); they fought to do away with multiplied standard by sleeping with partner of their choice and having children in unmarried partnership just to prove to men they are able to serve the child as father and mother. (Peyper, Klerk W, & Spies R, 2015)

According to (Nielsen L, 2012) a father-daughter relationships specialist in the USA, there are many unmarried women who believe that so long as a daughter has good and harmonious rapport with the mother, the father is unnecessary. Some choose to artificially become inseminated by anonymous sperm donors because they believe that fathers are not necessary for the wellbeing of their children.

The United States is leading the world in fatherless homes. Many children are being brought up by single mothers (Dickerson , 2014). Single motherhood is increasingly widespread in the United States. According to research conducted in USA, as many as 19 million children including youth adults do not know their fathers or are living in father absent homes, with most teenagers being raised by single caregivers or mothers (Gladys, 2020)

According to the Australian Bureau of Statistics, Single parent families are growing very fast and in an alarming rate (East L, Jackson D & O'Brien L, 2016)Most families are predominantly headed by women; hence there is a good number of children and adolescents given birth to by multiple partners and hence many children grow up without fathers at homes (East, Jackson, & O' Brien, 2016) . Absentee fatherhood is very predominant in Asian countries like Japan, many children grow up without their fathers (Gladys, 2020). In Africa South Africa is leading with almost half of the children growing up without father at home. (MUTEGI1 C k, Ndolo u, & . MWALW'A S, 2017), Namibia rank second after South Africa with high rates of father absence in Africa (Richter L, Chikovore J.& Makusha T, 2013).

Over 25% of households in places like Trinidad and Tobago, Cuba, Puerto Rico, Ghana, Kenya, and Rwanda are headed by women. (Kimani E, & Kombo K, 2010) In Kenya, father absence is equally a challenging and a rampant phenomenon (Ogola F. Maithya M & Makungu R, 2018)

Absentee fathers in kenya

"Something is very, very wrong with the Kenyan society. I met up • with four beautiful single women about 30 years old. Each has one or two children. None is married. All are seeking a partner but nearly giving up. Each is stunningly gorgeous and working. What is the problem? No insults?" Maureen Wang'ati-Gnagb April 5,2021 *https://twitter.com/scstourswild*

Since 1970, the rate of single parenting has increased from one in ten families to one in three families in Kenya (Magangi A, 2018)

Globalization and western influence is exerting impact on the role of fathers. Due to globalization, alternative methods of raising children that where never there before are springing up. With the changing times, there is an abdication of paternal responsibilities and Kenyan traditional way of fatherhood (Larcher A M, 2007)

Family formation has changed dramatically. Cohabitation has replaced marriages as the preferred first union of young adults. Pre-marital sex and non- marital childbearing have become increasingly acceptable and common place; and divorce rates have escalated at very high levels. Kenyan parents have become so preoccupied in the pursuit for wealth that being present to their children has become a huge challenge (Magangi A, 2018)

On Madaraka day, 1st June 2022, President Uhuru Kenyatta lamented the rise of single parenthood in the country with the following words:

The change face of Kenya family is captured in the census of 2017 it shows single parent family rose from 21.1% in 2009 to 38.2%... If this phenomenon is not arrested, it will cause a lot of havoc to the fabric of Kenya family and member of the society. (WAIRIMU M, 2013)

CAUSES OF FATHER ABSENCE

There are several factors that causes father absenteeism in families The most mentioned include: Divorce, Separation, Infidelity, having children out of wedlock, Work related issues, Business, Denial of Paternity, Death, Migration, violence, Abandonment, AIDS, Civil wars, Poverty and Unemployment, Imprisonment, Desertion, Substance use Disorder, Abuse of alcohol (MUTEGI1 C k, Ndolo u, & . MWALW'A S, 2017),

Divorce

Divorce render children and parent apart and mostly from the father. With almost half of all marriages ending in divorce, the phenomenon of a father absence in his daughter's life appears to have risen. The ripples of divorce seem to hit the children the hardest, especially the daughters (Mancini L, 2010)

Divorce usually results from factors such as domestic violence or when the father's drug use reaches the point that the wife cannot tolerate him in the house any longer. Domestic violence leads to female-initiated divorce, and the kids often suffer the most. The kids must grow up without their father.

(MUTEGI1 C k, Ndolo u, & . MWALW'A S, 2017), ...Asserts that that single parenthood is increasing in developed countries where divorce is more common unlike in the developing countries where there is not much divorce. In some African countries like Kenya what is common is the abandonment of family member by males because of unbearable poverty. Many people don't go in for divorce because it involves a lot and one needs to spend a lot of money to file in the case and process it until the end. Many couple opt for separation in most cases the women who lives with the children and the man elsewhere.

Denial of paternity

Rejection of paternal responsibly is always the result teenage unplanned pregnancy. This phenomenon of disputed pregnancy or Denial of paternity usually takes various form. Most men who are involved always exonerate themselves by expressing disbelief about the news of pregnancy and sometimes they relocation and rejecting responsible. The effect of this denied paternity affects the mothers and children throughout their lifetime. Some mothers have constant and unresolved distress cause by this denied paternal responsibility. Some considers it as a punishment for being careless, not taking contraceptive. Other effects on mother and children include the illegality of the child's citizenship. Difficulties for the child acquiring a legal access to his father. In some cases, some mother never discloses the true paternal identity to their children resulting in the child's resentment and confusion and an endless and unpleasant search for true identity of their father. (Nduna M, 2014)

Rural-urban Migration

Urbanization and modernization have over laden most families causing men to migrates into cities in search for Job. As a result, many families in African are left fatherless. According to (Magangi A, 2018) Kenyan parents have become so preoccupied in the pursuit for wealth that being present to their children has become a huge challenge.

In the traditional African society children rearing was shared by members of the family. And a family constitute extended family, several generations of cousins, uncles and aunts living in a compound or close to one another. Within this arrangement the children occupied central place and were well taken care of in a close family group. However, the rapid urbanization has altered the family structure. The modern era family has shrunken to a nuclear one consisting of father. Mother children depriving the care and assistance once receive from the extended family.

Out-of-wedlock Births

A leading cause of fatherlessness is out-of-wedlock pregnancy. In most cases people engage in premarital sex without the intention of getting married or having a child. Quite often when this irresponsible act result to a child, the father disappears leaving the baby with the young lady as a result the child grow up fatherless.

In south African according to (Patel L & Mazembo , 2016) if a man sires a child out of wedlock he is required to pay Intlawulo' is word for the payment of damages or 'fines' to the woman's family for fathering a child out of wedlock. These payments are understood to be reparations for having offended and disrespected the female partner's family by impregnating her out-of-wedlock. The cash amount to be paid is determined in a negotiation process between the two families and usually depends on what the male family can afford. In order to claim the right to access to one's child born out of wedlock. Sometimes fathers' inability to pay damages may result in their being excluded from involvement in their children's lives.

Incarceration

Incarceration of the father looms in the lives of many African-American families. Incarceration happens to fathers whose criminal activities necessitate their immediate incarceration. Being in prison deprives the father the chance to spend time with his children. Sometimes the child might visit the father in prison, but that time is never enough to establish a father-child bond. As a result, the child still feels fatherless. In other cases, the mother denies the children a chance to visit the imprisoned father, fearing it may cause the child emotional harm. If the child assumes prison is not a dangerous place, he or she may engage in crime just as their father did. When the mother denies the child the chance to visit the father in prison, it breeds a state of fatherlessness for the child

Materialist Constructions of Fatherhood and Masculinity

(Patel L & Mazembo , 2016) Writing about south Africa where there is an exceptionally high number of absent father says Overemphasis on the provider role by fathers and high expectations from mothers and societies is one of the reason why most fathers has disengaged them from their children. In a society wherein both masculinity and fatherhood are strongly associated with being a provider, father. In a context where women are impatience with fathers, where women get annoyed with father because they are not financially well-off or fail to provide. In a society where father is bared by the child's mother or her family from having access to the child because there are unable to make material or financial contribution to the child's life.

In a context where female partners and their families often only related to fathers as 'ATMs' (Automatic Teller Machines i.e. providers of material and financial resources, while ignoring other functions they can play in their child's life, practically and emotionally. In such a society where men find themselves pressed and Caught up in difficult economic circumstances and are unable to live up to all these expectations it seems easier for, many fathers to retreat from their children's lives. than to face the humiliation of feeling like a failure.

Unemployment and Poverty

The materialist perception of fathers accompanied by long-term structural unemployment and the persistency of mass poverty is a significant contributing factor in father absence. Unemployment and poverty constitute significant barriers preventing fathers from being fully engaged in their children's lives (Patel L & Mazembo , 2016) against this backdrop, 'an unemployed father who is unable to provide for his family tends to feel emasculated and unable to fully assume the role of a father. Unfortunately, unemployment is a widespread phenomenon. Many men in cities are likely to hold low paid jobs it is likely that many unemployed fathers live in poverty even their children and families also live in poor communities and social environments that reflect a high level of marginalization from the modern mainstream economic. Due to unemployment and poverty many father retreat from their children because they lack financial capacity to provide. A man who is unable is provide losses his title to be a father.

High cost of bride price

In Africa the complicated cultural traditions account for the reasons why fathers desert their children. According (Mavungu M ,Thomson H &, Mphak k, 2013), previously Marriage may be delayed because of the difficulties and high cost of negotiating arrangements between families. Bride price can be very high. In the past payment was in kind and a man could pay about 11 cattle. Today bride price can be paid in cash amounting to "several thousand US dollars. This amount is negotiable between the two family involved in the process. Sometimes the demand for this payment is done

without considering the rampant poverty and high unemployment rate that prevail in the contemporary society. In addition, some families take the advantage of this cultural practice to self-enrichment themselves by demanding exuberant amount of money and expensive gifts. Such a practice of asking for high price is considered as commercialization of bride wealth.

(Patel L & Mazembo , 2016) writing about South Africa. In the present time, there is still exist remnant patriarchal traditions (bride price) payment practice. The high cost of bride price which is a significant factor in lowering the rate of marriage and prevent men to be husbands and fathers

Relationship difficulties

Father absence is often closely linked to the quality of the relationship between the parents (or former partners), especially after a divorce or a break up. Conflict- ridden relationships, desire for vengeance after the collapse of a relationship, resentment, and lack of proper communication, often result in fathers' restricted access to their children or complete exclusion. Dysfunctional and conflict-ridden relationships have an effect on a father's ability to be present in his child's life. When mother of the child and father have a conflict the mother uses the child as a manipulative weapon to punish and exclude the father from accessing the child. some of these conflict often lead to suicide and murders. There are many recurrent media reports of children and female partners who have been murdered by the father and (former) partner because of child custody issues. Another factor that may contribute to the mother, grandmothers and extended family denying the fathers access of their children is the anger and negative behavior manifested by fathers.

Desertion

Desertion by fathers is often prompted by their inability to bear the burden of being primary providers. Marriage is determined by the financial power of the man. Being able to live together as partners or to be married is primarily determined by income. Quite often men in the highest earning category are three times more likely to be living with their children, than men in the lowest income category. The burden of failure becomes intolerable for those who lack the capacity to generate enough income as uneducated and unskilled laborers. Desertion is not always physical; it can also be emotional. The failure and shame when men feel when they cannot support their children, many being out-of-work, may cause men to avoid being involved with their children. (Richter, L , Chikovore & Makusha,T, 2013)

HIV/AIDS-RELATED MORTALITY

Of the South African men who are estimated to be fathers, approximately 50 percent do not have daily contact with their children. Data from national surveys across the period 1993 to 2007 suggests that father absence is increasing, partly because HIV/AIDS-related mortality is increasing (Richter, L , Chikovore & Makusha,T, 2013)

Finally, the preceding causes that have been discussed may not be the only contributors to father absence were it possible to explore the views of all fathers, women and children on this issues list will be different. (Mavungu M ,Thomson H &, Mphak k, 2013)

Impact of Father Absence on Daughter's Relationship with Men

63 % of suicides originate from fatherless homes; 70% of juveniles in state-operated institutions come from fatherless homes;

80% of rapists motivated by displaced anger grew up in fatherless homes;

40% of all children in the country do not live with their biological fathers;

85% of children with behavioral problems come from homes where the father is absent;

90% of homeless children originate from fatherless homes;

and 71% of children who do not finish school have absent fathers ⬦ (Herbert Z & Gadzikwa P, 2017)

The effects of fatherlessness manifest themselves in different ways including psychologically, socially, economically, spiritually, sexually, morally, and even physically. (Smith K A, 2017)

A daughter's positive, affirming relationship with father is a buffer to a variety of negative outcomes, such as early sexual initiation, teenage pregnancy, dating, violence, and risky sexual behavior, binge drinking recreational drug use, greater marital satisfaction, reduced fear of intimacy and increased comfort with her own Sexuality. Fatherless daughter experience difficulty in establishing and continuing intimate relationship with men. They experience, fear, rejection, abandonment, and commitment. They may develop masking techniques like 'overcompensating' in loving relationships by doing too much or overachieving too much. Many experience emotional pressure contributing to violence, drug abuse, early sexual activity and Antisocial behavior. Some absent father daughter experience difficulties in establishing realistic view of men in general realistic expectations and good judgement of life partner (Smith K A, 2017)

"A girl abandoned by the first man in her life forever entertains powerful feelings of being unworthy or incapable of receiving any man's love. Even when she receives love from another, she is constantly and intensely fearful of losing it."21 Fatherless daughters grow into fatherless women who strive to cover their wounds from the world with masks of perfection, over achievement, heightened sexual desire, or anger (Barnes, 2020)

Hurtful feeling for father's day celebration

"I hate father's day and here it comes again, every year in June, before school is over the teacher tells us to we are going to prepare something for father... my mother doesn't really like to talk about my fathers it makes her sad it makes me sad to when I thinks about it"

According to (Mancini L, 2010)most father absent daughters are very hurt inside many and resort to writing anonymous letters memoirs and poems online to release their pain of father absence .Here with some excerpts from some letters

In the first letter the young woman expressed how she wants her absent father wherever he is to know that he has hurt her more than anyone in this world could ever done. She goes ahead saying when she was sick and needed someone to share with, when she went for her first date and needed someone to share with, her father was nowhere to be found. Only her step dad was around. Her step dad has taken upon the fatherly duties to correct her when she goes wrong, to praise her to be proud of her to hug her, to celebrate with and for her when she graduated high school with a series of A's in her report card. She goes ahead saying the reason she is thinks of this things and sharing with him is let her absent father where ever he is to know that he has hurt her more than anyone in the worked deserting her. She goes ahead asking her absent father some question: What if she is now having a boyfriend or a husband what if she is now married s is his father aware? What if she is now having a child does her father knows that he is now a grandfather? What if she now wants to wed? who will walk her down the aisle and give her out? Wouldn't her like doing this things, like walking her down the aisles? She ends the letter saying she is now an adult and she needs to allow things of the past and move on with her life. However, she is still in need of father daughter relationship with the absent father if only he is willing her well and good. Finalizing she says all what she has expressed are just things to reflect about.

In the second letter the young lady among other things pose the absent father this the following: Why will you have children and allow your own personal issues in life to taint and destroy your relationship with them, she goes ahead saying she is not really sure what made her father abandon her. She goes ahead saying as time is passing and she is growing old, instead of becoming bitter about the situation she is becoming more empathic toward her absent father. She thinks of the lines: "Absence makes the heart grow fonder" but she doesn't and can't miss her father because he abandoned and never gave her the chance to know him in the first place

The third lady in her website she says there is no one in her life that she can call dad and that, dad is her least used word. She has never talked or mentioned about his absent dad to anyone none of her friends has ever heard her speak about him,

Lastly another lady said her absent father made her desperate for men's attention, she was in desperate need to feel love to fill the void and make up the gap left by her dad. Men often too advantage of her and often she filled the void left by her dad with sex.

All these letters provide a glimpse of fatherless women's mind it show how important father's involvement is to the daughter's life. Many daughters have written about their chaotic lives attributing their absent and irresponsible father as the cause.

Suicidal tendencies

Absent fatherhood in young people provoke the risk of suicidal tendencies. A research carried in South Africa revel that several factors contribute to this behavior. Some of the factors are family and social issues. One of the effect of lack of father figure is suicidal behaviors. Since such children lack a father figure with whom to share their problems they are prone to feel depressed manifesting suicidal thoughts. Some of the youth because they are raised in fatherless homes and feel rejected are predispose to get involved in anti-social behaviors. Often because many of these young people perceive themselves as unworthy, unwelcomed and unloved this provoke suicidal thoughts in them, Suicide is a cry for help due to emotional neglect from a single mother struggling to provide for the family. Some of these young people see the struggles of their mother as their fault, they perceive themselves as a burden to their mother and increase their likelihood of committing suicide(Gladys, 2020) Just to intensify this ideas (Varney Wong A., 2019)Women who grew up fatherless have a sense of inner void and attempt filling this void in some ways. such women may be prone to suicidal thoughts and feeling a great number of those who commit suicide are from fatherless home. Suicide is a way to destroy intolerable bad aspect of self

Overachievers or underachievers

Some absent father females have the impression that might be they were abandoned, by their fathers because they were not good enough. worthless useless and incompetent, with this idea in mind the invest a lot interest in further studies they aim to achieve they aim to achieve not only bachelor but masters and PHD degrees. They do this to prove to their fathers who abandoned them that they are as unworthy, are valueless as they might think and they are not as worthless as they thought. This to attract their love and attention .On the other hand some female becoming underachiever might be because of lack of love motivation from their absent fathers they are satisfied with diplomas and bachelor degrees they show no interest in further studies. (Zulu, 2014)

Eating disorders

Women from absent father's home are more likely to develop eating disorder: Anorexic or bulimic. Anorexia is a disorder characterized by refusing to eat enough to maintain body weight and an obsessive fear to of gaining weight. Anorexia may or may not be accompanied by bulimia is an eating disorder characterized by restricting food intake for a period of time followed by overeating or binging. Some father absent ladies presume that may be they were abandoned because they were not measuring up to their father's expectations might be the father was uncomfortable with her womanly appearance. With this thinking they seek to achieve perfection in their appearance in all other aspects of lives in order to please their fathers. Consequently, some diet excessively in an attempt to regain her former appearance as a little girl they do this to reinforce a cultural belief that women must be excessively thin in order to be considered attractive. The daughters may feel that losing weight will make her father happier force him to resolve the problem in their relationship (Nielsen , 2012)

Superwomen attitude

Girls who grow up without paternal involvement often deal with father loss by either becoming too loving and dependent on others or by alienating themselves from others. Some get involved in searching for a "perfect man" or attempting to become a superwoman": a woman who can do all that a man can do. A woman who does not need others or does not need . (Larcher A, 2007)

Fatherless women use perfectionism to cover up their wound. They resolve not to allow anyone to discover their wound. Perfectionism conceals her true identity and from revealing her real self to others. Fatherless women have a hard time forming and sustaining platonic or romantic relationship considering that a significant quality of relationship is transparency. The father rejection experience has distorted their insight some unrealistic standards and expectation about life and relationship

Some of them begin acting like a superwoman who can handle everything without help from anyone. They become overachiever with the motivation to prove to their absent fathers that they are able to make it without him. (Barnes, 2020)

Lastly according to (Allgood S, Beckert T,& Peterson C, 2012)Girls who have fathers involve in their life and upbringing have a less rigid stereotypical views of gender roles

Vulnerable

It is upheld that the way a lady behaves with the opposite sex is reinforced by the knowledge she acquires interacting with her own father. Therefore, women who were raised without fathers never had the opportunity to develop these traits. They are not sure about the dynamic between a man and women because they had no father figure as model, they had not witnessed of this kind of relationship. This lack of render them vulnerable to exploitation from men. (Zulu, 2014)

As adolescent some of these absent father women become obsessed and desperate for heterosexual relationship. They become overly dependent on men who take advantage of them. (Larcher A, 2007)

As some are vulnerable they get exploited by men others because of fear and mistrust originating from being abandoned by their fathers they tend to distance themselves from men hence develop negative attitude toward men. Such as fear or rejection, mistrust of men, lack of respect of men. Some due the lack of fatherly love do not think that a loving and intimate relationship with a man is possible. (Zulu, 2014).

Identity crisis

Fathers always play an important role in daughters' lives. There are
• many things that are learned and taught from fathers. It is a first
male-female relationship and she gains first reflection of herself as a
female who is discounted or valued, and then she gets acceptance and
self-respect. (Zia A & Masoom S, 2014)

A Fatherless daughters conceive herself as unlovable and unworthy.
Most fatherless daughters believe they are the reason that their father
left. Since they never receive father's approval they are prone to
question their self-confidence studies report that the way a girl's
perception of her father's feeling toward her had a lot of influence on
her. (Barnes, 2020)

Individuals desire knowledge of the background they need to know
where they come from where they belong. This knowledge helps
understand his/her self and give one a sense of identity. When the father
is absent this sense of belonging and identity is lost contributing to a lot
of problems in one's social relationship. ((Larcher A, 2007)

When children reach adolescent stage where the sense of their
identities is awakened they begin to get curious about who their father
is (Koketso M, Jabulani M , Lehlokwe S & Mafa P, 2019)

The knowledge of one's father gives him or her an identity and
boost their self-esteem and sense of self (SHUMA S, 2018)

Father is key to the child's indemnity. The father's surname to the
child symbolizes the child's connection to her family members and
ancestors. In some cultures, these ancestors are believed to be the

source of prosperity, protections good fortune and success (Zulu, 2014)

The knowledge of father gives one the sense of belonging at some point in no one wants to identify him/herself with your family knowing you're your family where you come from completes the puzzle in one's life. In terms of character. family history. Predisposition to personality disorder and some chronic illnesses (Makofane M, 2015)

❧

BEING CONSIDERED FATHERLESS generates in children a sense of loss, sense of loneliness, a feeling of stress and a great deal of confusion. Given that children take their clan's name from their father, an acknowledging biological fatherhood, is a manifestation of lineage, and it is important element of identity development (Koketso, Calvin, Lehlokwe, & Mafa, 2019)

No matter the outstanding recognitions or achievement of a young lady the presence of father absences places a young lady in a fix about the full picture for her life. A lady loses focus and direction when the father is absent this is because sometimes is considered a solid point of reference and foundation and anchor for a child's life. The search for father is associated with the search for herself (Schwartz J, 2003)

Displaced anger

Due to the fact that some youths from fatherless home perceive all men as their abandoning father they are likely to generalize and displace their anger toward them. These young people often fall into the temptation of either blaming themselves for the father's perceived abandonment or the blame other men. Some of them believed that they were abandoned by their fathers either because they were not good enough or adorable so they resort to blaming their significant other or their mother for their perceived father's abandonment. Because some youth struggle to understand the lack of father involvement in their lives. Some of them battle with impulse control or burst into anger in the midst of their significant others at any slightest disagreement. Battling with the perception that they were abandoned by their biological fathers they are also struggling establishing and maintaining intimate relationship with others They have abandonment issues that manifest in their paranoid preoccupation with fidelity in relationship and inability to commit themselves. Some of the youth people because they have unresolved issues with themselves they have the habit of suspecting their romantic partners of infidelity or having extra-marital without have a tangible proof, (Gladys, 2020)

Feeling unloved

According to (Jackson L, 2010) women with unknown / undisclosed Fathers always create a fantasy image of their fathers and for years they spend time searching for an intimate relationship that can fulfill this fantasy. Such women always feel that there is a chunk of themselves that is missing, thereby creating a void that only a father can fill.

(Zirima & Princess G, 2010) equally states that this search and yearning for a father leads some ladies into dating older men in order to fill the void that was left by their fathers in their lives ,some date older men for financial support, some have more male friends than female friends due to paternal absence. In addition, (Zulu, 2014) states that research laments the trauma of fatherlessness among children, children who grow up with absent fathers feel unloved, grieved, hurt and very resentful of their fathers. Such children are fun of phrases like "he wasn't there for me and "he was never there for me" just to stress to her father that she took note of his non-involvement and unavailability in her life.

Rejection feelings

Women who were raised without fathers have a sense of heighten expectation of rejection. (Barnes, 2020)

Absent fathers have impact on a child in the sense that when a child feels rejected by the father he/she may also expect rejections from others just as the father reject him .This rejection also makes the child feel a sense of unimportance which generates self-doubt. (Gladys, 2020)

Since fatherless daughter fear being abandoned the are very analytical in relating with people they put a lot of hard work and effort in relationship. This much effort invested in relationship may sometimes result in some of being too controlling over critical and displaying trust issues. (Barnes, 2020)

A child sees the absenteeism of a father as rejection and a feeling of being unloved. A lady with an unknown father does not only carry the heavy burden of an emotional scar and resentment but also, she has deep-seated unanswered questions of her paternal lineage as there are times every individual wants to identify their family to have a sense of belonging. Without a father, a daughter is left wondering if she is valued and worthy of affection from other where her father cannot be traced there is a hole in her heart, her personality thread is raptured. Knowing your pattern and family and where you come from completes one's life in terms of personality character and important of all medical history (Makofane M, 2015)

Many fatherless daughters commonly ask themselves and their mothers questions such as: where is my dad? Why did he leave me?

How could a father leave her child? Was I not lovable and good enough? In response to some of the questions such as "where is my dad?" some mothers are very polite and ensure not to say anything bad about their former partner, but they encourage their daughters to look up to their grandfathers, uncles who loved to protect and give them unconditional love, as a replacement and father figure in their lives. On the contrary some mothers who had issues with their former partner, refuse talking about them to the children. Understandably because out of frustration of the broken relationship they could give the children a very biased view of the father (Jackson L, 2010)

According to (Terwogt M, Reijnders, C J & . Hekken ML, 2002)to When the children realize that "the father' topic with mother is provoking embarrassment or aggression the children quickly learn that it is a topic to be avoided unless they want to risk or invoke punishment. Some children therefore decide to remain alone with a well cherished fantasy image of the father or choose to discuss this topic with other children or other family members. In some instances, where mother fail to reveal father's true identity children go into depression some get confused, bitter and may lead them to endless serious search of the that biological father, with some search leading them to an unpleasant discovery of a father who had moved on with his life.

Trust and security issues

Children who grew up without father figure often battle with a trust issues with themselves and with the world. When children grow up learn how to trust their parent who satisfy their desire and basic needs. They feel loved and valued but when children grew up in fatherless home lacking intrinsic trust they feel unworthy of love due to the lack of affection they experience from in their upbringing. (Gladys, 2020)

According to (Jackson L, 2010) women with unidentified and undisclosed fathers have a lot of struggles and challenges linked to fatherlessness, a host of them get stuck in life struggling with issues of trust and security. Because they did not get love and trust from the first man in their life (father) they felt deprived of a stable relationship with an adult male in their lives. The love for a father that was missing can't be replaced by the love for or of a mother or anything else, be it social work, friends, teachers, money, or well-designed public policies devised to help her. Many of such girls invest a lot of energy trying to overcome these struggles.

Negative view of men

It has been discovered that the world views of a daughters are significantly shaped by the presence or absence of the father. A father gives them a masculine example A father determines how their daughters view life and themselves; when a relationship with the father was encouraging and affectionate, a girl will view the opposite sex with confidence and dependence. If the representation is pessimistic, the girl will view the opposite sex with apprehension and distrust. From the father daughter relationship, girls form an expectation of how they will be treated and valued by men (Zirima & Princess G, 2010)

Girls who grow up without father involvement have the perception that men are untrustworthy As adults such ladies become obsessed with relationship with the opposite sex in search for a substitute (Larcher A, 2007)

Several researchers have also proposed that the mothers of father-absent girls teach their daughters to distrust men based on their own experiences (THORNE D R, 2001)

Unworthy for marriage.

Ladies who grew without parents, show negative attitudes towards relationships in its totality and reject marriage as they struggle to trust and respect men in addition to experiencing difficulties in accepting love and commitment from a man. The reasons behind some father absent females having difficulties in long term relationships with men may be the factors behind their paternal absence (Zulu , 2014).

Some researchers (La Guardia AC, . Nelson J A & Lertora I M, 2014) recounted that daughter with absent fathers feel disengaged and misunderstood. A daughter gains her first reflection of herself as a female who is cheap or valued and then she gets acceptance and self-respect. Growing up without a father in their home is disruptive to the father and daughter relationship and caused the daughters to have hurt feelings and a lack of respect for their fathers, also children born out of wedlock are often stigmatized as illegitimate by society. This may make them feel lost, unwanted and unloved.

With regards to this (Smith P, Khunou G & Taulelac M, 2014)observes: In the African 'traditional' setting children normatively take the father's character but with father absence, paternity name might not be acknowledged by the mother and her family. (Ndunaa & Jewkes, 2012) Concludes: young people who do not have an existing and consistent connection with their fathers are vulnerable to negative consequences as many of them reported feeling lost and unwanted.

According (Makofane M, 2015) to families with absent fathers are "not ideal marriage material" a general belief among Africans that a woman whose father was absent from home can't be married. In

African families, some parents deter their children from espousing females from such relations. The dread of parentages originates from the probability that some of these womenfolk may not have had part imitations to perceive the message and interaction between the parents.

Seeking validation from men

An anonymous letter of a lady who grew up with absent after "I was desperate for male attention any attention and men's interest in my body was the easiest avenue to being notice. How desperate l was to feel love to fill the void or make up for really attention and love l was missing from my father. I tried to fill my need with male attention and sex" (Mancini L, 2010)

When a female grows up in a father present home she easily receives love and validation from her father. On the other hand, girls who grow up in father absent home may begin to seek love, affection and validation from other male or individual who are available in most cases what is viable is sex. Many of such girl get early sexual experience and end up with broken heart (Glenn S, 2018)

. (Zulu, 2014) confirms this when he says "Because of the insufficient fatherly love that father absent young females receive; they may illustrate a yearning for male attention and affection". The yearning may lead the young women to be vulnerable to exploitation from any male who demonstrates attention and affection towards them. Some women confess to making poor decisions based on this vulnerability where they end up with older men trying to seek affection and attention from a father figure.

The idea of father absent daughters seeking older men is again highlight by (Zirima & Princess G, 2010)who notes that women who are abandoned or whose fathers divorced their mothers largely dated older men in order to fill the gap that was left by their fathers in their lives some dated older men for financial support, some have more male friends than female friends due to father absenteeism. This could also lead to prostitution just to fill the gap of left by an absent father.

Marrying older men

Women who grew up without a father may specifically search for this reassurance from men. This search comes from a desire to be accepted by men, as she has not felt this acceptance by her father oftentimes, this sense of acceptance is achieved through promiscuity.

According to (Peyper, Klerk W, & Spies R, 2015), daughters who experience abandonment from their fathers seek more attention from men and have more physical contact with boys than those daughters from intact homes. Female who grew up without a strong father figure attempted to be close and communicate with other males to fill what they were missing with their own fathers.

(Zulu, 2014)confirms this when he says: Due to the insufficient fatherly love that father absent young females receive; they may illustrate a yearning for male attention and affection .The longing may lead the young women to be vulnerable to exploitation from any male who demonstrates attention and affection towards them. Some women confess to making poor decisions based on this vulnerability where they end up with older men trying to seek affection and attention from a father figure Some women confess to making poor decisions based on this vulnerability where they end up with older men trying to seek affection and attention from a father figure... The idea of father absent daughters seeking older men is again highlight by (Zirima & Princess G, 2010)notes that women who are abandoned or whose fathers divorced their mothers largely dated older men in order to fill the gap that was left by their fathers in their lives. Some dated older men for financial support, some have more male friends than female friends due to father absenteeism. This could also lead to prostitution just to fill the gap of gap.

Resilience and capacity to overcome adversity

Father Absence does not necessarily need to result in negative outcome because absences affect people differently and depends on reasons of absence. In addition, there are some powerful single mothers who are good models and can teach, inspire and instill in their children the skills to be resilient to the victimization due to fatherlessness. They instill in the children adaptive coping mechanisms, financial autonomy and responsibility, personal strength, and financial independence. (Zulu, 2014) Some fatherless young women resort to coping mechanisms they develop persevering and self-reliant qualities. Although they realize that they need support they strive to be strong and independent. Other invest themselves in helping abandoned babies and street children as a means therapy and self-soothing. Some volunteer in playing helping in charity organization. Other school going who realized their self-esteem depend on higher grades placed emphasis on achieving higher grades hence becoming great academic achievers (Varney-Wong A, 2019)

PRONE TO STRESSED

The quality of father daughter relationship is also associated with the likelihood of her becoming clinically depressed. Women who feel rejected by their fathers are more likely to be clinically depressed. These women often isolate themselves avoiding romantic relationship because of fear of being rejected or abandoned. Most of them don't feel deserving they fear getting hurt in relationship. They fear getting into a relationship that might lead to heart break (Nielsen L, 2012)

Father absenteeism generates a lot negative feelings in both mother and child. Raising a child without a father in the picture can be very tedious "Parenting should be a two people task so that it does not have to feel like a burden. It becomes hard at times that you think of their father who never took responsibility:

There is a sense of loneliness and a feeling of stress. When children from absent father homes talk or ask about their father one can tell that the issues in not sitting well with them. Some often regret voicing the idea that if their father was in the picture the will be having no worries. The child and mother are stressed due to lack of insufficient funds. The absent father leaves a gap and the single mother struggles alone meeting the basic needs of the family (Koketso, Calvin, Lehlokwe, & Mafa, 2019)

Reiterating the issues (Glenn S, 2018)says Stress has been recognizably present when the father leaves the home or when the father has never been present in the child's life. When the father leaves the home, the mother is left to raise the child or children on her own, unless she has some type of support system that can provide assistance.

Family related behaviors are also worth considering. Several studies have shown that children from single-parent families are at increased risk of bearing children out-of- wedlock, marrying as teenagers, and becoming teenage parents. Besides being stressful in their own right, these Condition are associated with limited occupational attainment and welfare dependency. Children of divorce are also more likely to see their own marriages end in divorce than are adults from intact families of origin and previous research has demonstrated that divorced and separated individuals have lower levels of psychological well-being than do married individuals. These considerations suggest that people who grow up in single-parent families have more psychological problems in adulthood because they are more likely than other individuals to be single parents, have poor quality marriages, or be divorced. (Amato P, 2016)

High level of risky sexual behavior.

One symptom of fatherless women syndrome is sexual healing factor. Women who received little or no paternal involvement are more likely to seek to feel this void by seeking male attention and sexual intimacy. In relationship these women always seek to be in charge of the ways of engaging in intimacy

They seek physical closeness and confuse love for lust hoping it will fill the void of their hearts. If a man does not fill the void of their hearts they insist on have a baby with the hope that it will satisfy their desires. (Barnes, 2020)

Several studies show that children from single parent home are at risk of becoming teenage parents bearing children out of wedlock and marrying as teenagers (Amato, 2016)

When a father leaves a family for whatever reasons the children are deprived of a custodian of discipline, direction, a rule maker the one who provides law and order. When they grow in fatherless home they have a lot of unsupervised time due the lack of two parents, such females are easily liable to get involve in early risky sexual behaviors, alcohol, drugs and crime. Children's idea about sex is also influenced by parents if the father is not present definitely the mother is engaging sexually with someone to whom she in not married. This attitude may give the child the impression that sex I a very causal act (Schwartz J, 2003)

Shy away from men

Young ladies from absent father homes feel worthlessness, in emptiness, and ineffectiveness and often doubted themselves regardless of good performance and constructive feedback from others. (Peyper, Klerk W, & Spies R, 2015)

A fatherless daughter may shy away from males completely as she is unclear of how to relate to them or intermingle with them. This is a confirmation of the attachment theory that states that; among insecurely attached adults is the avoidant attachment, which occurs in individuals who had consistent yet unresponsive caregivers as infants. Often avoid forming relationships with others under the presumption that they will not get their needs met for fatherless women, this often means avoiding romantic relationships altogether (Castetter C, 2020)

Lack of confidence in socializing

Interacting with the father, a daughter may get to understand the male-female bond shaped her sexual style, a daughter's confidence and her sense of worthiness to be loved as a result of her father's loving involvement in her life. Father's love contributes to daughter's confidence and in her own femininity and sense that she is worth loving. A women's sense of confidence in later relationships and her sense of love worthiness is linked to her father. Daughters who had fathers particularly involved in their lives are less likely to seek for male love or male consent or even get involved in early sexual activities, childbearing, and divorce (Jackson L, 2010).

Fathers influence the social and sexual aspects of daughters' lives. Social development includes self' confidence in relating with peers, the ability to make friends, communicate well with peers, resolve difficulties with others and not being overly dependent on external approval and self-worth. Social development also includes the sexual and romantic aspects of her life, her relationships with boyfriends and with her spouse. Daughters who have secure loving relationships with their fathers are most likely to create emotionally close relationships with other men in their life. In order to create emotional intimacy, she must learn to communicate openly and honestly with men to resolve differences, feel comfortable, disagreeing and expressing her own needs and expressing anger and disappointment in inappropriate ways, she must learn to be herself rather than withholding or abdicate herself in intimate relationship with men. Daughters with good relationship with their fathers are more likely to rely on their boyfriends for comfort and to feel secure in relationships. They are not as fearful of and less distrustful of men. Overall father generally has more impact than mother on daughter's romantic relationship; some daughters are more concerned about their father's opinion about their boyfriends than their mother's opinion. Daughters think mothers will find their boyfriends physical unattractiveness more unacceptable than fathers will. On the other hand, fathers will pay more attention on their boyfriends' social and pecuniary status and his inability to make good income more unacceptable than mothers. (Nielsen L, 2012)

Feeling unwanted and stigmatized

In some society where children are humiliated for being fatherless, the lack of father in the family is considered a stigma a mark of social disgrace and this generates in the child destructive negative feelings and a sense of loss (Kevorkian C, 2010)

According to research fatherless children or children born out of wedlock are looked down by society .They are often considered as illegitimate and this cause many of such children are vulnerable for they often report feeling lost and unwanted (Smith, Khunou, & Nathane-Taulela, 2014)

SOME AFRICAN PARENTS dissuade their sons from marrying ladies from absent fathers' home because there is a belief among Africans that girl children without parents may not stay long in relationships with men. Such women raised in homes with absent father are not ideal marriage material and in addition some ladies with absent fathers loath and distrust men (Makofane M, 2015)

Feeling reluctant to make romantic choices

Ladies from father-absent homes have difficulties in forming relationships with men. They are prone to be reluctant around men or may be sexually violent. Father-daughter relationship served as model for daughters to learn how to interact and be accepted by men. (La Guardia AC, . Nelson J A & Lertora I M, 2014)

Without a father figure to aid as an exemplary leader of how she should be treated, women may choose poor romantic partners for themselves. The existence of father imparts to their daughters on how they should be handled by their partners. As result, women tend to choose romantic partners that have similar characteristics to their father. Furthermore, hypothetically owing to the detail that the broods who come from stable families are discouraged to marry those who come from a broken family on the supposition that they may not be stable in marriage. There are many reasons for this conception, some because girls who grew up with single or no parents may be problematic.

Also, the girls from fatherless households may begin dating far earlier than their peers. If the father's absence is due to divorce, the girl's unmarried mother may be dating around in search of a new companion. As a result of this exposure, the young girl may copycat her mother's behavior (Castetter C, 2020)

Women who saw their fathers as being affectionate and approachable were found to date men who were also able to form a close, comfortable relationship with others. Those women who saw their fathers as being emotionless, distant, or inconsistent were not likely to be dating men with those same characteristics they did not discover any connection between men's interactions with their fathers and the partners they chose. The men's choice of partners was influenced by how they viewed their mothers (THORNE D R, 2001)

Depressive symptoms

Children response to parent's lost different. The loss of a parent can bring untold distress to a child it can even affect his or her perception toward life. Death of parent makes a child realize and understand that life is not just games and fun. (Farooqi R & Khan A, 2021) Children who lost their father by death are affected differently from Children who lost their father through divorce or negligence for they can endure with the understanding that death is an act of God. However, some females whose fathers have died may become introverted and develop depressive symptoms (Singh R, 2004)

The parent's death means growing up and understanding that life is not just fun and games Existing literature indicate the significant the variety important role a father play is a child's life; eg the father is a moral guide, a bread winner, a protector. a companion and care giver. Studies indicate the death of a father affect a daughter drastically. The loss of a dad affects a daughter emotionally and psychological in fact the wellbeing of the daughter is affected at all levels

After the loss of father, female adolescents encountered drastic changes in the life course. This dramatically impacted their well-being at all levels including psychological, emotional, and mental. Daughter goes through self-esteem issues, grief, anger, remorse and resentment, some daughter experience seclusion and low self-control.

Some become liable to negative and psychological disorder they manifest hopelessness, deficient self-esteem and hypersensitivity (Farooqi R & Khan A, 2021)

Daddy issues!

Daddy issues is a 21st century popular media term used for challenges that inevitably come along with the lack of a father figure from one's life, particularly a female's. This phenomenon is known to affect women differently, and debatably more drastically. (Castetter C, 2020)

Complaints of those with these issues nearly always include problems with entering and maintaining close relationships, the feeling of not belonging, feelings of having little control over one's life and problems with making decisions in life. All of these complaints point to the presence of underlying identity problems .Often the client him- or herself actually says: "I don't know who I am." Clients appear to be engaged in a search process (which some formulate as the search for oneself, and others as the search for their unknown father (Terwogt M, Reijnders, C J & . Hekken ML, 2002)"

Another name for daddy issues is Fatherless Daughter Syndrome

This syndrome has four symptoms that are overlapping and have psychological and social implication on the live of fatherless daughters. These include "Un" Factor, Triple Fears Factor, Sexual Healing Factor, the "Over" Factor, and RAD (Rage, Anger, and Depression).

The first symptom "Un" Factor influences a woman's self-perception: The fatherless daughter frequently believes she is unworthy and unlovable. She has concluded that she is the reason her father abandoned her. Women who did not receive their father's approval as children are more likely to doubt their own abilities.

A girl's perception of her father's feelings toward her has a greater influence on her self-esteem than anything her father does or says. The "Un" factor manifests in a woman who has low self-esteem and self-worth. "No one would want her; no one could love her," she believes. With such a low self-esteem, she believes she is unworthy of happiness, love, peace, respect, or dignity.

This type of woman is preoccupied with high anxiety but low avoidance. . She has an exaggerated desire for closeness but lack trust in others' availability and responsiveness to her needs. She relies heavily on the approval of others for a sense of personal well-being, but is fearful of being rejected or abandoned

The belief surrounding love that corresponds to this mindset is that love "needs to be earned, so they had better perform. As a result, if they are missing something, they try to locate it. It is Dad's love in this case. If he isn't available, they look for it in every man they meet."

The second Fatherless Woman Syndrome is the Triple Fears Factor, also known as abandonment syndrome. A woman with the triple fears factor symptom is motivated by fear. She is most afraid of commitment, rejection, and abandonment in a relationship. To keep her fears from becoming reality, she begins to over-analyze her partner and their relationship. This woman frequently chooses men who are unable to commit to relationships, treat her poorly, or are emotionally unavailable.

The third symptom is the Sexual Healing Factor.

This factor is most visible in intimate relationships. In a girl or woman, sexual expression can be a primary indicator of fatherlessness. Women who received little or no attention from their fathers are more likely to fill the void by seeking male attention and sexual intimacy.

When it comes to relationships, this woman must be able to control how she engages in intimacy. She may mistake love for lust in the hopes of filling the void in her heart and experiencing physical closeness. If a man cannot fill her empty heart, she insists that having a baby will provide her with the love she craves.

The fourth symptom is the "Over" Factor. When a woman uses perfectionism to cover her wound, she exhibits the "Over" factor. She is determined that no one, man or woman, will discover her wound. Perfectionism robs her of her identity, enveloping her in shame and preventing this fatherless woman from revealing her true self to others. This misconception leads her to believe that no one will like, want, or love her for who she is, so she creates a false exterior. Women who feel rejected by their fathers struggle to maintain relationships, whether platonic or romantic, because one of the most important aspects of a relationship is transparency. Instead of focusing on herself, this woman will begin "acting like a superwoman who can handle everything without anyone's help. She is regarded as an overachiever. Her motivation for success is to silently prove to her father that she is capable of succeeding without him. If that fails, she turns to substances to help her cope with the pain of failure.

Where's my daddy?

"**Y**esterday was father's day and we got to celebrate fathers. But single mothers where do you tell your children their father are?" from a radio presenter.

Have you ever asked your mother the whereabouts of your absent father?

During adolescence, youngsters are usually observed to start asking questions around their father's identity as this is seen to be a time when the requirement for family belonging and identity starts to become strong Father absent children are at times described as feeling 'illegitimate', and unlike 'legitimate' children who know their biological fathers. It is assumed that there may be confusion around identity and legitimacy during the adolescent stage for children without fathers Therefore some children without fathers feel embarrassed to talk about their absent fathers to their peers as it may elevate personal issues about their identity and legitimacy.

"Where's my daddy?" I cannot count the number of times I asked my mother this question. Further, I am certain that this is the very same question that millions of fatherless little girls have asked their mothers.

Many girls due to rejection feelings oftentimes ask themselves and their mothers questions such as: where is my dad? Why did he leave me? How could a father leave her child? Was I not lovable and good enough?

"My mother said she is "waiting until the right time" to tell me"

"I am three years old when I first ask my mother, "Mommy, where's my daddy?" My mother responds with politeness and does not bad mouth my father, nor what I later perceive to be his devastating and decimating abandonment. She says, "You have Papi Lencho [my grandfather] and Tio Rigo [my uncle] and your cousins who all love you and who you can look at like your daddies." So, I had several fathers. Men that I "adopted" as a "daddy" and who in turn gave me unconditional love and protection. However, this 2 love did not fill the emptiness of not having a relationship with my biological father" (Jackson L, 2010)

"...I am avoiding my mother...so I am avoiding the fact that when she sees me crying she would want to find out why, then I would say it's because my father...That's what I hate whereas she raised me alone up to this stage so I think she would ask why am I only asking about my father now..."

"*Sometimes you feel like asking the parent that you currently stay with, in my case my mother but you also have that fear and find that you are unable to ask such a question so that's what is really bothering me...I just lock myself in my room thinking that if Sometimes you feel like asking the parent that you currently stay with, in my case my mother but you also have that fear and find that you are unable to ask such a question so that's what is really bothering me...I just lock myself in my room thinking that if my father was around things would have been different so I do cry sometimes but not loud...When I see other [young] females don't want their children to know their fathers then I ask myself if that particular woman knows the pain that the child will go through because I know it from experience...I am here without the knowledge of who my father is...*"

...My girlfriend came to visit me at my home and my mother saw her and asked me if we knew each other, I said yes. She said that 'it is good that kids of the same father know each other...if your father was still alive he would be very happy to see you together'...the girl and I had no clue what she was saying about 'your father'... {incest was a pathway to discovery of true paternity}

... each time I asked, my grandmother shouted or beat me..." for asking about information she heard from the street. She said: "...By the time I asked I needed to confirm something that I already knew, I needed to hear it from an adult...from my own family... so I gave up..."

"...Last year here at school they were asking us for school fees, R400...She [mom] said she did not have money...I asked her 'what about my father where is he? You once told me he is a teacher'...

What follows is a car conversation between a little girl who ask the about her absent father.

Little girl: where is my daddy

Mother: which daddy

Little girl: My daddy

Mother: which one? which one?

Little Girl: My daddy, mom

Mother: mmm You are coming here... you are amazing me

Little girl: Mom l want my day

Mother: Are you not wearing clothes?

Little girl: I am

Mother Did you not eat

Little girl nooo, crying....

Mother who said you should no eat? the fridge is full of food

Are you not wearing a cap for the raze of the sun?

Little girl: I am

Mother: I am you father

Little girl: No you are my mother

Mother: this one is testing me l will slap you; You go back to where your daddy found you

In the depth of Hitler

Little girl: screening: I want to know my daddy

Mother; yeeh yeeh you are coming here you are talking to me the way you want you are coming here yeee you are forgetting; you have grown because of me. eeeh l am your father that you are looking for. I am your father

Little girl: you are my mother

Mother: I did so much to you this child is testing me. I did so much to you eeh when you were sitting like a child l was wiping you, you were crying like a baby there

Little girl: l want o know my father? Where is my father?

Mother; MMmm you do you want to know who your father is?

Little girl: yes, I want to know who my father is

Mother? Do you want to know who your father is?

Little girl: Yes

Mother: You came out of thin air even me l wasn't expecting you eehh like this you just jump, you just jump I don't know who your father is no idea. Me l don't know; I don't know who your father is? You jumped like air you jumped. I picked u up out of nowhere. Did you hear me say pay electricity in the house? You are living for free and this is how you test me. where is my father? where is my father? You are knowing English here because of me

Little girl crying ... I want know who my father is ....

Mother: you know who you fara fara father is I am your father the son and the Holy spirit Thats your father, the son the father and the holy spirit: if you want to **know** your father read the bible Please you are testing me. You are testing me eeh are you asking because its father's day?

Little Girl; nooo Mother if you are asking because it father's day? Write God a letter that is your father.

Little girl: since l was young l didn't know my father.

Mother: how are you going to remember your father when you were one year and six months?

Get off my car go look for your father;

Amondi Aroko Loise Kim,: urged *women to be honest with their children and tell the truth about their dads who abandoned them*

.The gospel artiste said there is no point in lying about the absentee dad and instead, mothers should let their kids know they raised them because their dad ran away Her followers were left with mixed reactions with some differing with her sentiments on telling kids the truth

"The child of an absent father may have confusion about who his father is and why he is not around The more information he has, the better his social and emotional well-being .Father-absent children often fantasies about their father frequently believing that the absence is their own fault .In such cases, one of the roles of psychotherapy is to create a more realistic appraisal of the father" (O'Dwyer D, 2017)

The sting of absent fathers

In an online site called Exprienceproject.com fatherless daughters have published anonymous letters and memoirs about their chaotic lives and their pain of rejection citing their irresponsible or absent fathers (Mancini L, 2010) Below are some excerpt from those letters

DEAR DAD

Even using that word brings up images of pain, lonely nights and years of questioning why I wasn't enough for you. While I am working to forgive you and my mother for being human, the question remains: How on earth could you abandon me?

I needed you to help balance out my female-dominated life, be there to give me the talk about boys so that I wouldn't have to suffer through my current state of bad relationships and empty voids. I taught myself how to ride my bike, had a first boyfriend my mother had to interrogate and when I became a debutante I needed you to be there to dance with me down the isles instead of my grandfather. You were supposed to be the first man to tell me that I'm beautiful and help me to know myself before anyone had the opportunity to label me. I was supposed to be your "little girl

A man that puts himself last does not abandon his family. What would you have lost by being in my life? I wasn't a troubled child. I ate my veggies, became class president and even put myself through college. Your minimal contribution is an insult to who you could have been to me.

I'm sorry that you missed out on something and someone so great. But I guarantee that I won't let your actions break me. I pray for my husband to be the father to my children I never had. That my daughters know the comfort of their father's arms, his voice, his love, his care.

One day I'll walk down the aisle without you again by my side. But then again I'm used to it. Thank you for the pain because without it I wouldn't know healing, I wouldn't know love, I wouldn't know God.

DEAR DAD
All those times I cried for you, you never came
Out of all the sports I played
You never showed up at one game
All of the awards I received
I never heard you clap
You were never there
For me to sit on your lap All the times I fell
and scratched my knee
You were the one who wasn't there
To comfort me
All those times I was bored
and wanted someone to call
You still weren't there
Not there at all
I always tried to make you proud
Hoping you would love me more
but you never seemed to care
So what did I even do it for
You weren't there for any of my firsts
Might not be for any of my lasts
It's like you're not here in my present
Just like you weren't there in my past
I try to move on
But no one knows how hard it is
For your own father not to love you
As much as he loves his other kids

But I hold my head high
To keep things from looking so bad
But deep down I still wish
I had love from my dad
(poem by Jacqueline M. Smith)

Feeling and thoughts of fatherless children

These feeling and experiences and drawn from scholarly research works they comprise experiences at home, experiences in school, and experiences in neighborhoods and they all anonymous

"I had many thoughts going through my mind: "He left me. He really left me. Why would he leave me? Wow, I guess I am not good enough for him since he left me." From this point, I was never the same. My father wounded my heart. The void created in my heart allowed for rejection to take residence, causing me to search for someone or something to fill the emotional and physical void of my father.

"Over the years, I learned the art of wearing a mask. I found myself putting my softer side away and allowing my anger and toughness to become my protector. On the inside, I nursed a broken heart, but on the outside, I was strong. I vowed to protect myself from being hurt again; I kept people at a distance. No one knew that I was searching for validation, acceptance, and love. I put forth the effort to be the best in school, church, and sports so that I was always receiving validation from someone. Perfection was the mask I used to hide my sadness and disappointment. I refused to be a weak individual. With these suppressed emotions, I found myself lashing out in anger towards people. I used my mouth as a weapon to hurt others when I felt attacked or threatened. I wanted people to feel the same way I did on the inside. (Barnes L, 2020)

"You always have that one parent that's strict and you have to do this, you have to do that. Always stay on top of your schoolwork. And it wasn't my mum. I knew it was my dad because my mum was the nice one and

the lenient one. But my dad was the strict one and "get things done" type of parent. I didn't have him so, all right, just took advantage of my mum...I didn't have to do homework. I didn't have to listen to teachers. I just wasn't very disciplined. (Participant 16

"I had really bad grades. My grades were all dropped after my mom had them split. After that, my grades dropped really bad. I ain't going to lie, I was doing good at first but they dropped really bad and it just put me through a lot of stuff as I got older. I started becoming of course like you said, I was still I don't care-ish, but I was also sad but I just didn't express myself to people. (Participant 19)

"Depression. I didn't want to do my homework. Just wanted to spend time by myself...Anything I did particularly reminded me of him, because he would be the one 83 that would help me with my homework and the absence was really [affecting]. (Participant 7

"I guess it affected it because most of my friends have two parents in their house. I guess it affected it because I felt like I was looked at differently or not as. Most of my friends in school basically had better cars, better clothes. Education-wise it was I don't know. It was pretty normal. It wasn't too bad. I can't say that I got bad grades because he wasn't there. I can't say that I got good grades because he wasn't there. (Participant 11)

"When I was a child, it seemed like we had to struggle for different things. We really didn't have a lot of support. It just didn't seem like a home life that I saw on TV, that's something that I wanted. It just affected the structure of us having things that we needed. My mom had to work real hard and we really didn't have anybody else there.

"As a child...I saw my mom struggle a lot because she did a whole lot and my father really wasn't there, so I think it affected our home life just in the sense that we didn't have two parents to go to the activities where dads were supposed to go. My mom was always the one to go. And home was, I mean home was difficult because all we have was my mom and doing those difficult, like teenage years and as a child, she had to handle pretty much us and take care of everything. So that took a toll on us and I learned to be

independent like her and help her with the dishes and help her around the house. As a young child, I think we learned to learn responsibility early.

"I think [my father's absence] affected the home life because the father just wasn't there to be that father figure, per se, and to be the head of the household. As we know, men should be the head of the household and control things. It was a whole lot more work on my mother because I think my other siblings felt the same way, that mom was the mother and the father because he wasn't there. The father wasn't there. I think it had a tremendous effect on the family to know that daddy wasn't in the house. (Participant 6) (Brown S, 2018)

"...sometimes when I think about my father I feel empty; I feel as if I lack something as he left us when I was still in primary school". "I really feel the gap of not having him around". ".... some of the times I will be thinking about him during lectures...I find it difficult to concentrate when I start thinking about my dad". "It was not easy being separated from my father at such an early age...I feel distressed when I think about him".

"I am angry with my father because he left us when we needed him most....i do not think I will be able to forgive him"

"...I believe if my dad was around I wouldn't be so distressed by some life events such as heartbreaks the way it affects me now...I am sure he would be supporting me".

"I think having a father was necessary because some of my friends had their dads, so l wanted to have him just as them, I'm sure having my father around would help to know where I come from, my relatives and to know where I really belong to".

"I hate fathers' day and here it comes again, every year in June; before school is over the teacher tells us to we are going to prepare something for fathers... my mother doesn't really like to talk about my father for it makes her sad and it makes me sad too when l thinks about it" (Simon, 1983).

"Filling forms that requires you to mention your father is very uncomfortable or directly being asked about your father, you have to say,

'I do not know', or 'is dead' or something, you feel excluded' (23-year-old male participant)

"I use my mother's name and always wonder who am I? I do not know what I will tell my children if I do marry."

"You need to have a sense of belonging. One day I was writing my mom's name on my desk calendar and my friend said, 'Is your dad so bad that you do not write him on your desk calendar?' I got so angry (22 year old female participant) (Tshweneagae, 2012)

I am thinking of getting married in the near future, but who will negotiate my marriage? Who would I tell my wife is my father, how would I answer if she wonders about my ability to be a proper father because I have never known one? (25-year-old male participant).

I do not know who to blame – I dated a girl and went all the way only to hear rumors that she was my sister. I no longer date. I feel like a social misfit (24 year old male participant) (Tshweneagae, 2012)

⌘

"SOMETIMES YOU FEEL like asking the parent that you currently stay with, in my case my mother but you also have that fear and find that you are unable to ask such a question so that's what is really bothering me...I just lock myself in my room thinking that if my father was around things would have been different so I do cry sometimes but not loud...When I see other [young] females don't want their children to know their fathers then I ask myself if that particular woman knows the pain that the child will go through because I know it from experience...I am here without the knowledge of who my father is...

"There is a real fear of asking mothers about fathers' identity in a bid to avoid conflict"

"Single mother should learn to not involve their kids in hating on their father simply because things did not work our well between themselves. I wish my mother had just told me the truth about my dad

Social experiences

"... I have coped with life without him and this made me to have more male friend that the female ones". "as a girl, there are some things that I expect to have for instance clothes, money and laptop my grandmother could not afford all those stuff, therefore it affected me as l was depending on other people's things for me to cope with university life"

"...I have always felt that dating an older guy is good for me because they always take care of me the way my dad would have done....

"....my social relationships were a total mess, I had multiple relationships and unproductive social life"

> *With my dad not being in my life, I kind of have an idea of how a man is supposed to treat me, but...I really don't know what to do, what not to do, what's acceptable and what isn't acceptable in a relationship. So...I don't really know what a good relationship is, or what one is supposed to be like. I have only seen the bad: like when my mom talks about my dad and says, 'He's not a good father and he was never a good boyfriend, either.' I just go off what I see in the movies because I don't really know. So, I feel like my relationships end because I have these high expectations of what I think relationships are supposed to be like, and then they're not*

"I do not trust men and I have a fear that they will desert you if you depend on them. This has affected me in such a way that I prefer to be independent and I find it hard to appreciate even if a man do[es] things for me in good faith."

"I feel that I cannot put all my trust in men, i.e. guys I go out with. I make sure I never rely on anyone for survival, even when we are not dating anymore; I must still be able to continue with my life and never feel like a part of me is gone or stagnant. "

"However, I am unable to be in a stable committed relationship with men. I don't allow myself to fall in love with them because I am scared that

I will not be able to handle a heartbreak which in my mind is inevitable for people that fall in love, and also have a fear of them leaving me once I get comfortable.".

"when my father passed on I was in form 2, I then grew up with my mother, I have since grown to be self-reliant, I have learnt to work hard in order to get what I want"

, "we grew up without a father because he abandoned us, our mother taught us that we should be able to stand up for ourselves since we have no father, ...I never knew my father, as such, my mother is also my father"

" It has not negatively impacted my perception on men because we had uncles, who were morally supportive of us, our pastor at church also played a father role in our lives, so that has helped me not to think that all men are capable of what he did to us, but I am angry with him in particular."

"I have never had a bad perception about men and I continue to look at men positively, except those who abuse women and children. Generally, I seem to have a great view of men and I am raising one and I endeavor to instill good values in him."

".....maybe I would have been able to go to better schools and get better education"; "It was very hard for my mother to raise the school fees that was required hence I was affected greatly"; ".....my grades are always fluctuating," "I haven't been to the schools l desire"; "...if my father was alive I was going to fulfil my wish of going to an international university"; "There are some things I want to do in my life but the fact the l cannot approach my grandmother freely it will affect my goals in my life"

.... he was the bread winner and the only male present in my life";

"He was not necessary because he did not care and provide for the family";

...he was the financial provider and also supported us emotionally"."...they are some financial problems my grandmother is facing that my father could have solved if he was alive" (Zirima & Princess G, 2010).

Stop running away with children from their biological parents and families when your marriages or relationships don't work. You can be separated, but still be there for the kids. STOP THE TRANSFER AGRESSION! Stop blocking kids from their family that cares and loves them. If the person you left loves the kids and wants to be there for the kids, let the person be there for the kids. If the family of the person you left, loves the kids, and wants to be there for the kids, let them. It's about the kids! If you truly care for the kids, let them know their family. Stop the transfer aggression! This nonsense is becoming out of control and kids are getting tripped in the middle. Some kids don't know their uncles, aunties, cousins, and relatives because one parent blocked them from knowing. It's sad! May God guide kids who are victims in this type of situation to grow up, search, and locate their families in Jesus name! May the heartless parent who do this to the children never go unpunished! There is God!

WHY ABSENTEE fathers impact DAUGHTERs MORE THAN SONs

Only girls have the super power to leave home, family and their surname to live and adjust in a new home & family They are priceless. Respect Girls!

A panelist asked me the following question during defense of my aforementioned thesis: *Why did you choose to research on the impact of absentee fathers on daughters and not on sons?* Here you go: majority of previous studies have minimized the impact of fathers on daughters in comparison to mother-daughter due to a long-standing notion that fathers play a more important role in the development of sons than daughters (Allgood S, Beckert T,& Peterson C, 2012) Some believe that if fathers do not spend enough time with their sons, "the sons would become 'sissies' (Fienman B, 2017)

However recent developmental research reveals that father/daughter relationship has profound impact on daughters than mother/daughter relationship.

> Fathers generally have as much or more influence than mothers on many aspects of their daughters' lives. For example, the father has the greater impact on the daughter's ability to be confident, and to relate well to the male counterparts, well-fathered daughters are usually more confident, and elicit positive behaviors, and more successful

in school and in their careers than the former (Nielsen L, 2012)

There are various potential theories to explain the reason why girls of absent fathers are impacted more than boys. One of these theories is self-in-relation-theory, which proposes that the sense of self develops differently in males and females. A male's sense of self, according to this theory, comes about through gradual separation from the adults in his life. First he separates from the care of his mother, then from the rest of his family, and eventually from any mentors that have helped guide him. They achieve their sense of self via autonomy and independence. For women however, their identities are achieved through relationships with others. They tend to define themselves based on the quality of their relationships with family, friendships, as well as any other kind of relationship. Therefore, the lack of a father-daughter relationship for a girl may make her feel incomplete as an individual. (Castetter C, 2020)

"Girls are most affected by fatherlessness since it influences how they socialize. Men are biologically trained to be independent, so separation and isolation do not change them as much as it affects the girl child. The man can ignore feelings; the woman, on the other hand, obsesses about feelings, which leads her to behaviors such as staying in relationships too long and searching for "the perfect man." The girl may also attempt to become a "superwoman," effectively trying to pretend she does not love or need others for her survival. (Smith K A, 2017)

CAN a MOTHER teacher her Son how to be a man?

Can a Single mother teach her son how to be A MAN?

During one father's day when 1 was visiting my grandfather I attended with him, my parents and my sister. During the announcements portion of the service, the pastor asked for the eldest father in the congregation to stand and be recognized; my grandfather stood to receive resounding applause. The pastor then asked for the youngest father in the congregation to stand; my cousin's husband stood and received the same applause. Finally, the pastor asked that all fathers in the congregation stand to receive gifts that had been prepared specially for them on their day. Much to my surprise, many women stood up claiming to be both mother and father. This caused a great stir in the church, mostly laughter and affirmations of the dual role that some mothers play.(Thompson A, 2014).

Can a single mother teach her son how to be a man? Can a mother play the role of the father? A father cannot be a mother, and he should not try. From the beginning of the identity politics era, which is when women and men began to see each other as rivals, there's been a lot of one-upmanship over parenting, and who is the more important parent. In the public sphere, women won hands-down, but this has turned out to be a disaster for the millions of children who, as a consequence, grew up in broken, fatherless homes. Concerned men have responded to this by saying that they are every bit as good at parenting as women. Many have embraced the concept of equality, suggesting that women are no more capable of raising children than men. In a sense they are correct, as children raised by fathers seem to do better than those raised by single mothers, but they are also wrong in some regards. ....As men, we do not need to pretend that we can be mothers, nor should we want to

Raising a child is supposed to be a collaborating and cooperating task between both the mother and the father. The child needs both the father and mother to achieve full mental and emotional development. (Gladys, 2020)

No matter how much a single mother tries to perform the functions of both parents, the child benefits much more from having their father as an active presence in their lives. No matter how nurturing a mother we may have, there is still a significant need for a father in all of us. (Barnes, 2020)

Male children experience slower mental maturation, as compared to their female counterparts, as single mothers are more likely to pay more attention to female children, which is natural as being of the same gender they are conversant with their feminine needs; therefore, the presence of a male parent is essential in the process of nurturing the children, especially boy children. Nevertheless, when male children are raised only by their mothers, their development tends to be single sided; they need the same gender role model in order to emulate through modelling (Gladys, 2020)

Are you father's child?

S ingle-mother-parented households are a norm in sub-Saharan Africa and mothers "...give their last names to their children Nonetheless, as children grow, some question why they are using their maternal surname" (Nduna M & Jewkes R, 2010)

Although academic research on the importance of a father's surname is minimal. However, debate on the use of father's surname is important. Not only does psychological research seem to pathologies' not having a biological father, but from a traditional point of view disconnection from paternal ancestry is considered as a problem. The father's surname to the child is of importance as it symbolizes the child's connection to all members of her father's family including the ancestors who are believed to be the source of success and good fortune, prosperity and protection. Connection to the father's family is claimed to give the child her background, belonging, her roots, and therefore an identity (Zulu, 2014)

The used of maternal surname is considered de-cultured and inappropriate hence they disowned, undermined and invalidated the use of their mother's surname. The use of father's surnames in sub-Saharan Africa, carry a lot of significance in cultural personal identity, also problems around surnames seem to create a perpetual sense of dissatisfaction and feelings of disenfranchisement among some Africans (Nduna M & Jewkes R, 2010)

> *...the surname I'm using is not my father's because my mother was not honest with me...so I had to use my mother's surname*

and... This thing makes me feel...somehow... I can't even explain it to you..."

Children take their clan name from their father. Taking on a father's surname fosters a legitimate identity that gives a child access to their father, paternal uncles and family lineage. In some African societies traditional rituals, have to be performed on the father's side to introduce the child to their paternal ancestors so that the child can legitimately claim their paternal ancestry. There is a notion that one's father is the right person to preside over traditional ceremonies and rituals such as marriage processes One's father plays an overseeing role in rituals, and citizenship rights. the use of a biological father's surname is essential for registration for an identity document, passport, marriage and death certificate. The pursuit for using a biological father's surname is also motivated by seeking ancestral protection, some mothers, fathers, guardians and children believe that not using a biological father's surname could have negative repercussions for the child and may cause personal problems and bad luck. (Nduna M & Jewkes R, 2010)

Overcoming Father Absence

Despite all the factual evidence of potential developmental effects of father absence, growing up without a father does not indicate that a child is doomed. Children who grew up without the support of a father still have the potential to thrive and flourish. They are not destined for failure (Castetter C, 2020)

The absence of a father made some to realize that they should stand up for themselves in order to survive in life. This is because they feel they are compelled to establish and prove themselves (Zirima & Princess G, 2010).

Great persons in history have emerged against all the odds to overcome challenges encountered in leading a fatherless life, and they have shown the world that achieving their dreams despite the situation is indeed possible (Smith K A, 2017)

Father Absence does not necessarily result in negative outcome because absences affect people differently and depends on reasons of absence\ (Zulu, 2014)

In the absence of their fathers some more likely to have other insights; hence the challenges they have experienced because of the lack of resources that their fathers should have provided, result in them acquiring more life skills and oftentimes they work harder in life than children from two-parent homes It is believed that growing up without a father breeds self-resilience, as children learn to depend on themselves, rather than expecting too much from someone else. They are also likely to be wiser than their counterparts are (Gladys T R, 2020)

Much of the research regarding father absence revolves around patterns that have been found among those who have experienced it these patterns do not take into account the major variability among these individuals. In other words, nobody's circumstances are exactly the same and therefore everybody's developmental outcome will differ (Castetter C, 2020)

It is believed that growing up without a father breeds self-resilience, as children learn to depend on themselves, rather than expecting too much from someone else. They are also likely to be wiser than their counterparts are (Gladys T R, 2020)

A resilient person is one who has seen, heard, and experienced suffering while remaining competent and optimistic about the future. Individuals who are resilient are autonomous because they have a sense of their own identity, capability, and control over their environment. Some daughters without fathers may have strengths such as generic support and their own personality traits that improve their coping and competency despite the adversities commonly associated with growing up without a father. The resilience of these absent daughters may be influenced by their mothers. There are some powerful single mothers who are good models and can teach, inspire and instill in their children the skills to be resilient to the victimization due to fatherlessness. They instill in the children adaptive coping mechanisms, financial autonomy and responsibility, personal strength, and financial independence (Zulu, 2014).

Just because the child may not have a father present in their life does not mean they cannot benefit from the support of another male father-figure. In fact, the mother can play a huge role in mitigating the negative effects of father absence for her child. For instance, surrounding the child with alternate beneficial male role models like teacher and other family members. The mother can also avoid speaking poorly of the child's father. It is often tempting for mothers to badmouth their ex-husband and/or father of their child, however this does nothing but hurt the child. It can make the child feel ashamed, insecure, and uncomfortable (Castetter C, 2020)

Some fatherless females described themselves as survivors who needed to carry on with their lives whether their fathers were present or not. Some father-absent females appeared to be self-sufficient and estranged from their father's family (Zulu, 2014)

Some fatherless young women resort to coping mechanisms they develop persevering and self-reliant qualities. Although they realize that they need support they strive to strong and independent. Other invest themselves in helping abandoned babies and street children as a means therapy and self-soothing. Some volunteer in playing helping in charity organization. Other school going who realized their self-esteem depend on higher grades placed emphasis on achieving higher grades hence becoming great academic achievers (Varney-Wong A, 2019)

Making it without a father

"*I am making it without you, dad*" from a fatherless female student

The common assumption has been that children from father-absent families do not achieve success in life. However, many examples prominent people who have grown up in father absent families becoming productive members of society

The following are prominent world figures who have grown up without their fathers

Barack Obama Barack Obama,

The 44th U.S. president, offers a good example of a person brought up in a father-absent family who managed to live a life opposite of the destiny often characterized by children from fatherless homes. According to Obama, women have been the most important people in his life. He gives thanks in many speeches to his mother and grandmother, who devoted much effort to ensure they could provide for him and his two sisters. Obama seeks to appreciate his mother, Anne and praises her for encouraging him to pursue his goals in life. In a speech, while in office, he described his mother as heroic and said he owes his life achievements to her. Growing up without a father, he had few role models around him and ended up making many mistakes in childhood. Consequently, he explains that his mistakes allowed him to realize that life compromises values and morals that now guide him daily. On the same note, no father figure gave him direction in living right; he learned how to teach himself and develop values true to him. Similarly, he mentions that a fatherless family exposed him to the advantages of learning how to prioritize his issues. Nevertheless, Obama shares how he sought to fill his father's absence growing up and often wonders how his life would have been if his father were present. Moreover, he admits that being brought up without a father has influenced him not only to be involved in his own children's lives but to lend a helping hand to other fathers by contributing to communities that encourage fathers to spend quality time with their kids

Oprah Winfrey

A great personality who overcame the great difficulties and hardships of fatherlessness is Oprah Winfrey, an American media proprietor, actress, producer, and best known for The Oprah Winfrey Show. Oprah ranks as one of the richest African American and the greatest of all black philanthropists in American history. Oprah received the Presidential Medal of Freedom award by President Obama in 2013. Additionally, Oprah is recognized with honorary doctorate degrees from Duke and Harvard The great achievements of this African-American female persona were never served to her on a silver platter. Oprah was born in abject poverty in rural Mississippi to a teenaged single mother. Oprah was a victim to sexual abuse, and at the age of fourteen, gave birth to a boy who later passed away. Oprah describes herself as a promiscuous teen who, throughout her growth to greatness, made many unwise decisions not worth repeating. Oprah claims to have had a love affair with a married man who had no intention of leaving his wife; yet in the face of rejection, she wanted the man more. She claims to have felt depleted and powerless, pleading with the man, and her subsequent depression drove her to leave a suicide note to her best friend. She explains that the rejection she felt from the world made her weak and fragile. She endured abusive relationships to somehow find the approval she desperately needed. She felt useless and, in return, put herself in harm's way to seek significance in the world; smoking crack cocaine became part of her story, she regretfully confesses. However, Oprah's situation was a little different from those completely fatherless. Her parents separated soon after her birth and left her in the care of her maternal grandmother. At age six, Winfrey was sent to live with her mother, and at age twelve, was sent to live with her father; she was then put back in her mother's custody, and that is when the impoverished, urban lifestyle pummeled her with all its wrath. Repeated sexual abuse affected Winfrey the most. As noted earlier, fathers are the first men with whom girls identify, protecting and nurturing their intimate lives; yet the men around her abused Oprah. Remarkably, Oprah developed a love for spiritual nourishment quite early while living with her grandmother. At two years old, she addressed a church congregation about Jesus' resurrection on Easter day.

LeBron James

Another African-American personality who has beat the odds is professional basketball superstar LeBron James. He learned how to live by a teenage mother who struggled to provide for James amidst poverty. Fans worldwide can see James give his mother credit for his success; he refers to her as his champion. He acknowledges his mother's effort to raise money for his upkeep, which meant often moving to get a job. In a tribute to his mother, James thanks his mother for the person he has become. He credits her for exposing him to basketball and teaching him to be loving and caring. James also recognizes his mother's sacrifices and struggles as the key to his motivation and inspiration. On a unique side note, he also thanks his father for being absent as his absenteeism encouraged and challenged him to be a better person; James says that his mother filled the role of a father to him. James also thanks his football coach who helped fill the gap and provided the foundation of his basketball excellence. (Smith K A, 2017)

To all fathers. would-be fathers and absent fathers

F athers nurture your daughters throughout their childhood because the relationship will likely affect all their future relationships with men.

> **You're not just raising your daughter or son...**
>
> **You're raising somebody's wife or husband and somebody's mother or father.**
>
> **So... Raise them well!**

FATHERS:
Be your daughter's 1st
love. Open doors for
her, pull her seat out,
& talk to/treat her with
the utmost respect...
Set expectations on
how a man should
treat a lady, and she'll
never settle for
anything less.

DEAR MEN.

Close your eyes, imagine you have a daughter, Image she is dating a guy just like you Did to you smile? No Then change.

DEAR MEN

your sons will grow up to be like you. Your daughters will grow up and marry men like you Is that going to be a good thing or a bad thing

Half you men better pray your daughter never runs into a guy like you.

Dear men,

Treat your women with respect because one day someone will do same to your daughters.

Dear Men!

A father's job isn't to teach his daughter to be a lady, it's to teach her how a lady should be treated.

Dear men,

What make you a man is not the ability to have a child but the courage to raise one

Dear Men,

The first thing to ask a woman whom you just meet is her relationship with her father? If she doesn't relate well with her dad Or her dad deliberately avoids her Just forget about her.

Some African parent dissuade their sons from marrying ladies from absent father's home since the belief among Africans that girl children without parents may not stay long in relationships with men. Such women raised in homes with absent father are not ideal marriage material and in addition some ladies with absent fathers loath and distrust men. (Makofane M, 2015)

\

Positive self-talk for daughters with absent and unknown fathers

Thank you for rejecting me
thank you for bailing on me
thank you for not caring
thank you for not being there when I needed you
thank you for ghosting me
thank you for not making an effort
thank you for not treating me right.

*I needed to understand that your rejection was
meant to show me that my worth is greater and that
this redirection is meant to get me back on the track
you took me off of.*

-Kayil York

"YOU THINK L CAN'T LIVE without you? what do you think you are?? my phone charger?"

"Never be defined by your past. it was just a lesson, not a life sentence"

"It isn't where you are coming from. it is where you are going that matters". ella Fitzgerald

"If you don't hear what hurt you, you'll bleed on people who didn't cut you"

"Don't be upset when people reject you. nice things are rejected all the time by people who can't' afford them". the positive diaries

" Thankful for every rejection that led me to my breakthrough"

"Thank you for not being there when l need you the most"

" I went through my darkest times alome . sorry if l act like don't need anyone"

" Life goes on, with or without whoever and whatever. never for that."

" You are not the rejected one. you are the one who broke free"

"I promise you, somebody rejecting you is the univer protecting you"

" I didn't grow up having role models. i grew up have people l didn't want to be like and seein situations i never want to be in. not all of us are dealt the right cards but that doesn't mean you cant reshuffle your deck for a better outcome"

" And my story goes on. withou you" a seven word short story

"Ihank you for not being there for me when l needed you most. trust me, you are the one who taught me to not expect anything from anyone" sahil verma

Bibliography

Thompson A. (2014). *Fatherhood from their Voices: Discovering the Meaning of Black Non-Residential Fatherhood.* Georgia.

Brown S. (2018). *The Lived Experience of Daughters Who Have Absent Fathers: A Phenomenological Study.* Walden.

Castetter C. (2020). *The Developmental Effects on the Daughter of an Absent father Throughout her lifespan.* Merrimack.

Dickerson C,. (2014). *The Lived Expereince of fatherlessness in male adolescent , The student Perspective .*

East L, Jackson D & O'Brien L. (2016). *Disrupted relationships: Adult daughters and father absence.* Santa Barbara: Routledge.

Farooqi R & Khan A. (2021). *Exploring the Impact of Father's Demise among Female Adolescents.* Punjab,.

Herbert Z & Gadzikwa P. (2017). *EXPERIENCES OF FEMALE UNIVERSITY STUDENTS WHO GREW UP IN FATHER ABSENT HOMES.* Zimbabwe.

Kevorkian C. (2010). *Father Absence and Self-Esteem Amongst Economically Disadvantaged Children .* Rhode Island .

Koketso M, Jabulani M , Lehlokwe S & Mafa P. (2019). *PERSPECTIVES OF SINGLE MOTHERS ON THE SOCIO-EMOTIONAL AND ECONOMIC INFLUENCE OF 'ABSENT FATHERS' IN CHILD'S LIFE: A CASE STUDY OF RURAL COMMUNITY IN SOUTH AFRICA.*

Larcher A. (2007). *Hope for the fatherless?: A grounded interpretive approach* . Brigham.

Mancini L. (2010). *Father absence and its effects on daughters.*

Mavungu M ,Thomson H &, Mphak k. (2013). *So we are ATM fathers.* Johannesburg.

Nduna M & Jewkes R. (2010). *Undisclosed Paternal Identity in Narratives of Distress Among Young People in Eastern Cape, South Africa.* Pretoria.

Nduna M. (2014). *Growing Up Without a Father and a Pursuit for the Right Surname.* Johannesburg.

Nielsen L. (2012). *Father-daughter Relationship : Contemporary Research and Issues.* New York: Routledge.

O'Dwyer D. (2017). *A Psychotherapeutic Exploration of the Effects of Absent Fathers on Children.* Dublin.

Ogola F. Maithya M & Makungu R. (2018). *CAUSES OF FATHER ABSENCE AND HOW IT AFFECTS ACADEMIC PERFORMANCE OF THE BOY CHILD IN KCSE IN SUNEKA DIVISION, KISIICOUNTY, KENYA.* KENYA JOURNAL OF EDUCATIONAL PLANNING,.

Richter L, Chikovore J.& Makusha T. (2013). *The status of fatherhood and fathering in South Africa.* Durban.

Smith P, Khunou G & Taulelac M. (2014). *Are you your father's child? Social identity influences of father absence in a South African setting.* Johannesburg: Routledge.

THORNE D R. (2001). *FATHER ABSENCE AND ITS EFFECT ON YOUNG ADULTS' CHOICES OF COHABITATION, MARRIAGE AND DIVORCE* . Manhattan,.

Varney-Wong A. (2019). *AN EXPLORATORY STUDY OF THE INFLUENCE OF AN ABSENT FATHER on the Identity formation of women.* Cape Town: University of Cape Town.

WAIRIMU M. (2013). *PERCEIVED FACTORS INFLUENCING DEVIANT BEHAVIOUR AMONG THE YOUTH IN NJATHAINI COMMUNITY, NAIROBI, KENYA.*

Zirima & Princess G. (2010). *Experience of female university students who grew up in father absent homes.*

A, Skordas M. (1988). *The Impact of the Father/Daughter Relationship on Women in Educational Administrative Leadership Positions.* San Diego: Digital@sandiego.edu.

Allgood S, Beckert T,& Peterson C. (2012). *The Role of Father Involvement in the Perceived Psychological Well-Being of Young Adult Daughters: A Retrospective Study.* Utah .

Amato P. (2016). *PARENTAL ABSENCE DURING CHILDHOOD AND DEPRESSION IN LATER LIFE.* Nebraska: The Sociological Quarterly.

Barnes L. (2020). *Father Wounds in Black Christian W ounds in Black Christian Women: Their effects on Indentity and perception of God as father.* PORTLAND,.

EAST L , JACKSON D & O'BRIEN L. (2006). *Father absence and adolescent development: a review of the Literature.* London,: SAGE Publications.

Fienman B. (2017). *A Daughter's Perspective of Her Father's Influence on Her Parenting.* East Eisenhower: ProQuest.

Gladys T R. (2020). *The Perceived Impact of Absent Fatherhood: An Exploration of Young Adults'Experiences of Father Absence.* Natal.

Glenn S. (2018). *EFFECTS OF FATHER ABSENCE ON A THER ABSENCE ON AGE OF SEXU GE OF SEXUAL ACTIVITY AND CURREN AND CURRENT STRESS AND A T STRESS AND ATTACHMENT LEVELS OF Y T LEVELS OF YOUNGADULT WOMEN .* Kentucky.

Jackson L. (2010). *Where's My Daddy? Effects of Fatherlessness women on Relational Communication .* San José.

Kimani E, & Kombo K. (2010). *Challenges facing nuclear families with absent father in Gatundu North District, Central Kenya . An online journal of the African Educational Research Network.*

La Guardia AC, . Nelson J A & Lertora I M. (2014). *The Impact of Father Absence on Daughter Sexual Development and Behaviors:.* Huntsville, TX: SAGE.

Larcher A. (2007). *Hope for the fatherless?: A grounded interpretive approach.*

Magangi A. (2018). *Influence of Father Absence on Self-Esteem of Secondary School Students in Keiyo Sub-County, Kenya.* Eldoret.

Makofane M. (2015). *"Not all men are fathers": Experiences of African women from families with absent.* Petroria: Social Work(Stellenbosch).

Mancini L. (2010). *Father absence its effects on daughters.*

MUTEGI1 C k, Ndolo u, & . MWALW'A S. (2017). *FATHER ABSENTEEISM ON SOCIAL VULNERABILITY AMONG MODERN FAMILIES IN KENYAN URBAN HOUSEHOLDS: A CASE STUDY OF KIBRA COUNTY, NAIROBI,.* Nairobi.

Nduna M & Jewkes R. (2010). *Undisclosed Paternal Identity in Narratives of Distress AmongYoung People in Eastern Cape, South Africa.* Pretoria.

Nduna M. (2014). *Growing Up Without a Father and a Pursuit for the Right Surname.* Johannesburg,: Braamfontein.

Nielen L. (2012). *Father-Daughter Relationship.* New York: Taylor & Francis Group.

Nielsen L. (2012). *Father daughter relationship : Contemporary Research and Issues.* New York: Routledge.

Padi T,Nduna M, Khunou G, & Kholopane. (2014). *DEFINING ABSENT, UNKNOWN AND UNDISCLOSED FATHERS IN SOUTH AFRICA.* Johannesburg: Routledge.

Patel L & Mazembo . (2016). *'Children, families and the conundrum about men Exploring factors contributing to father absence in South Africa and its implications for social and care policies.* Johannesburg: Taylor & Francis group.

Peyper, Klerk W, & Spies R. (2015). *Experiences of young adult women with emotionally absent fathers.* Routledge.

Schwartz J. (2003). *THE EFFECT OF FATHER ABSENCE AND FATHER ALTERNATIVES ON FEMALE AND MALE RATES OF VIOLENCE.*

SHUMA S. (2018). *THE INFLUENCE OF ABSENTEE FATHERS ON DAUGHTERS WHOLISTIC DEVELOPMENT IN URBAN AREAS: A STUDY OF SELECTED INSTITUTIONS IN NAIROBI COUNTY, KENYA.*

Singh R. (2004). *A historical and an empirical survey of fatherhood.* Natal.

Smith K A. (2017). *A Study of Fatherlessness in the African-American Community in Relationship to the Positive Role of Christianity.*

Terwogt M, Reijnders, C J & . Hekken ML. (2002). *Identity problems related to an absent genetic father.* Budrich: Zeitschriftenartikel.

Tshweneagae, T. &. (2012). *Where is my Daddy? An Exploration of the Impact of Absentee Fathers on the Lives of Young People in Botswana.*

Varney Wong A. (2019). *Am Exploratory study of the influence of Absent father on the identity fomation of women.*

Zia A & Masoom S. (2014). *POSITIVE FATHER AND DAUGHTER RELATIONSHIP AND ITS IMPACT ON DAUGHTER'S INTERPERSONAL PROBLEMS.* Karachi.

Zulu, N. T. (2014). *I am making it without you, dad": fatherless .* Natal.

About the Author

About the Author

Fr. Mark Ndifor OFM Cap is a dedicated Catholic priest belonging to the Franciscan Capuchin Friars. With a profound commitment to serving his community, Fr. Mark has spent over two decades in priesthood, embodying the values of compassion, empathy, and service.

Fr. Mark holds a **Master of Arts degree in Counseling Psychology**, earned through diligent study and dedication to understanding the complexities of the human psyche. His academic journey also includes a Bachelor of Arts in Counseling Studies from the University of Manchester, as well as a Higher Diploma in Counseling Studies. He is a registered member of the Kenya Association of Professional Counselors, showcasing his commitment to upholding the highest standards of professional practice in his field.

During his academic pursuits, Fr. Mark delved deep into the intricacies of father absence and its impact on daughters' self-esteem. His master dissertation, titled **"Influence of Absentee Fathers on Daughters' Self-Esteem in Selected Colleges in Ruiru Sub-County,**

Kiambu County, Kenya," sheds light on this crucial subject, offering valuable insights into the challenges faced by young women in the absence of paternal guidance.

As Fr. Mark celebrates his 25th year in priesthood, marking a remarkable silver jubilee in his service to God and community, he continues to be a beacon of hope and support for those in need. His unwavering dedication to helping others navigate the complexities of life has earned him respect and admiration from all who know him.

Milton Keynes UK
Ingram Content Group UK Ltd.
UKHW050716010724
444982UK00014B/914

9 798224 387564